FUN
FEET

A Quantum Book
Published in 2016 by Search Press Ltd.
Wellwood, North Farm Road,
Tunbridge Wells, Kent TN2 3DR

ISBN: 978-1-78221-402-1

QUMMCLF

This book was conceived, designed and produced by
Quantum Books Limited
6 Blundell Street
London N7 9BH
United Kingdom

Publisher: Kerry Enzor
Editor: Philippa Davis
Design: Mike Lebihan
Editorial Assistant: Emma Harverson
Photography: Simon Pask
Production Manager: Zarni Win

Manufactured in China

9 8 7 6 5 4 3 2 1

Special thanks to the super-cute babies who starred in this book:
Sophie Bloom, Edie Gaskell, Oscar LeCouffe, Caitlin McGlynn and Freya Workman

30 super-cute booties to crochet
for babies and toddlers

Contributing Editor: ***Kristi Simpson***

Contents

Chapter 2: 42

Contents

Introduction

Imagine the smile on a new mum's face when she opens a gift to find the cutest pair of shark shoes, eggs and bacon slippers or even monster claw boots. I would be so surprised and delighted to receive them.

If you are new to crochet, don't worry, the Crochet Basics section (see pages 134–142) will guide you through reading the patterns, getting started and all the stitches you need. Give it a chance, it is easier than you think and so rewarding – you can even teach yourself! Many years ago my daughter received a crochet kit. I could have pinched my sister for gifting that to her because she asked every day for two weeks for me to teach her. I just didn't know how. Finally, I realised it came with instructions and just by looking at the step-by-step photos I taught myself and I then taught her. The funny thing is, I instantly loved crocheting. I enjoyed making something from just a string of yarn and I never stopped. I bet you will too.

I hope you enjoy this collection. It is fresh, creative and completely over the top fun! Whether you dress little feet up in Burger Booties or Sleepy Owls, your baby's feet will have the cutest creatures keeping them warm!

How to Use This Book

Choosing Your Pattern

The 30 patterns in this book are organised into chapters by theme: **Out of This World** contains a host of monsters and aliens; turn to **Wild Animals** for inspiration from the zoo of booties; choose **Cute Creatures** to be inspired by animals closer to home – woodland friends; or flick to **Good Enough to Eat** for truly delicious designs based on food.

You can also choose a project by skill level. Simply check the rating in the Before You Begin panel that comes at the start of each project. Skill levels are as follows:

- **1** Easy: uses basic stitches and techniques
- **2** Intermediate: requires use of some more complex stitches
- **3** Advanced: perfect if you are confident with basic crochet skills and ready to try some more exciting stitches and techniques

The Patterns

The patterns come in two sizes suited to 0–6 months or 6–12 months. All of the patterns use one of two basic sole templates or are worked in the round from toe-to-heel. You can find the step-by-step instructions for the soles on page 143.

Before You Begin

The Before You Begin panel for each project contains all the essential information you need before picking up your hook.

Skill Level Ranked 1 to 3, see above
You Will Need Lists the specific yarn(s) and colour(s) used to crochet the patterns, along with the hook sizes you'll need and any additional materials or tools required
Tension Always check the tension before beginning to ensure perfect results
Stitches and Skills A quick reference to techniques covered at the back of the book
Notes Be sure to read the Notes and any Helpful Tips before beginning a project

Crochet Basics

On pages 134 to 142, you will find a comprehensive guide to all the stitches used in the book, as well as tips on reading the patterns. Read through this chapter before starting your project to familiarise yourself with the stitches and techniques you will be using.

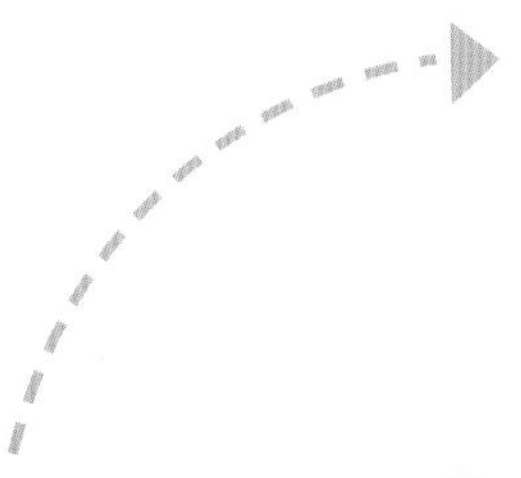

Meet the Designers

Kristi Simpson
Our contributing editor designs patterns for RAKJpatterns – a company inspired by her five children, which she runs with her husband from her home in the United States. Kristi is a member of the Crochet Guild of America, the author of *Sweet & Simple Baby Crochet*, *Mommy & Me Crocheted Hats*, *25 Cozy Crocheted Slippers*, *Happy Hats for Kids*, and *Sweet Shoes for Baby*. She has had her designs published in international crochet magazines. Find her at kristisimpson.net.

Patricia Castillo
Patricia is the crafter behind the blog popsdemilk.com where she shares her crochet creations. She likes to draw inspiration from cartoons, video games and her inner kid to design fun amigurumi patterns. With years of crochet practice on her hook, Patricia feels there is so much more to learn and is always in search of new challenges.

Lisa Gutierrez
Lisa crochets from her home in the United States, where she lives with her husband and two children. She loves to knit, crochet, sew and embroider, and is beginning to experiment with paper crafts. She shares her imaginative patterns at goodknits.com.

Xuan Nguyen
Xuan discovered and fell in love with the art of amigurumi in 2010 and has since made numerous creations, initially by knitting and then moving to crocheting. She started by sharing photos of her work on Facebook which led to the creation of the *Fat Face & Me* photoblog in 2012. A selection of her patterns are available at her Etsy store, *Fat Face & Me*.

Laura Sillar
Laura has been crocheting since childhood, and six years ago she discovered the fun of amigurumi. For the past couple of years, she has dedicated her creative talents to the craft of amigurumi, and is passionate about creating crochet designs and handmade toys. She lives in Estonia with her husband and two children. Find her designs at happyamigurumi.blogspot.co.uk.

Dedri Uys
Author of *Big Hook Rag Crochet* and *Amamani Puzzle Balls*, Dedri is passionate about crochet and shares her love of the craft through online patterns and tutorials. She lives in London with her husband, three sons and the family cat, where she also works as a therapy radiographer. Find her patterns on Ravelry at dedri-uys or follow her blog at lookatwhatimade.net.

Emma Varnam
Emma is the author of *How to Crochet* and *Crocheted Keyrings & Charms*, and designs patterns from her home in the north of England. A working mother and wife, she gains enormous joy and peace of mind from crocheting, and always has a project on hand to keep her out of trouble! Find her at emmavarnam.co.uk.

Safety Advice for the Baby Shoes in This Book
The projects in this book have been designed with little fingers and mouths in mind. Three-dimensional pieces are crocheted seamlessly or securely fastened in place. Buttons and other plastic components have been avoided as they can become a choking hazard. When making a project ensure that all elements are securely joined, and that there are no components that may become a choking hazard.

If crocheting for a very active baby you may want to make a nonslip sole. You can do this by making a suede sole for the bootie. Alternatively, sew a piece of elastic or trim to the sole to give a rough tread; there are also special stickers available from craft shops that you can use. Babies and toddlers should be supervised at all times when wearing booties.

OUT OF THIS WORLD

1

CHOMPER THE ALIEN

CHOMP CHOMP!

Chomp! Chomp! These frighteningly cute alien booties make a fun accessory for little space explorers. Try these ankle biters as a quirky twist to a party dress.

BEFORE YOU BEGIN

SKILL LEVEL
3

YOU WILL NEED
Cascade 220 Sport 50g (1.75oz); 150m (164yds); 100% Peruvian highland wool
1 in Magenta 7803 = MC
1 in Cotton Candy 9478 = CC1
Approx 23m (25yds) White 8505 = CC2
Approx 9m (10yds) Black 8555 = CC3

Hook
3.75mm (US F/5)
2.5mm (see note, page 135)
Adjust hook size if necessary to achieve correct tension

Notions
Stitch marker
Yarn needle

TENSION
11 sts and 8 rows in htr to measure 5cm (2in)

SIZES
0–6 months, sole length 9cm (3½in)
6–12 months, sole length 10cm (4in)

Note: Instructions are given for the smallest size first; the larger size is given in square brackets [ ]

STITCHES AND SKILLS
See Crochet Basics (pages 134–142)

Working in rows
Working in rounds
Working into front and back loops
Magic loop
dc2tog
htr2tog

To Make the Booties

(make 2)

Bootie

Using MC and larger hook.

Round 1: 8 htr into a magic loop, pull magic loop to close shut, sl st into first htr to join. (8 sts)

Round 2: 1 ch, 2 htr into each st, sl st into first htr to join. (16 sts)

HELPFUL TIP

When working in spiral rounds, use a stitch marker to mark the start of each round and move the stitch marker as the work progresses.

Round 3: 1 ch, 1 htr into first st, 2 htr into next st, *1 htr into next st, 2 htr into next st; rep from * 4[6] more times, 1 htr into each of next 4[0] sts, sl st into first htr to join. (22[24] sts)

Round 4: 1 ch, 1 htr into each st, sl st into first htr to join. (22[24] sts)

Rep previous round 3[5] times. Now work in rows.

Row 8[10]: 1 ch, 1 htr into each of first 18[20] sts, turn.

Row 9[11]–13[15]: 1 ch, 1 htr into each st, turn. (18[20] sts)

Row 14[16]: 1 ch, 1 htr into each of first 8[9] sts, htr2tog, 1 htr into each of last 8[9] sts. (17[19] sts)

Fasten off, leaving a 30cm (12in) tail. Fold the last row in half and whipstitch the edges together.

Re-attach MC at centre back. The edge will be worked in dc, in rounds that are joined, as follows:

Round 1: 1 ch, 1 dc into same sp. Next, crochet into the side of each row as follows:

*1 dc into side of first row, 2 dc into side of next row; rep from * 1[2] more times, dc2tog over side of next row together with first un-worked htr st, 1 dc into each of next 2 sts, dc2tog over next st and side of next row, work edging as follows: *2 dc into side of next row, 1 dc into side of next row; rep from * 1[2] more times, sl st into flo of first dc, switching to CC1 during sl st. (17[23] sts)

Round 2: 3 ch (counts as 1 tr), 1 tr into flo of same sp, 1 tr into flo of each rem st, sl st to 3rd of beg

HELPFUL TIP

Work sl st round (first round in white) loosely, to retain a stretchy cuff.

3 ch, switching to CC2 during sl st. (18[24] sts)

Round 3: *Insert hook through next st of Round 2 and corresponding back loop of Round 1 and sl st; rep from * to the end, sl st into blo of first st. Cont with teeth:

Teeth

*2 ch, sl st into same sp of Round 3, sl st into blo of next 3 sts; rep from * around, sl st into first st. (6[8] teeth)

Fasten off, weave ends into WS and trim.

Ears

(make 2 per bootie)

Using MC and smaller hook.
Round 1: Make 3 ch, dc into 2nd ch from hook, 1 dc into next ch, 3 ch, sl st into 3rd ch from hook, working on opposite side of ch, 1 dc into back of same ch, 1 dc into back of next ch.

Fasten off, leaving a 30cm (12in) tail.

Eyes

(make 3 per bootie)

Using CC3 and smaller hook.
Round 1: 6 dc into magic loop, pull magic loop to close, sl st into first dc, switching to CC2 during sl st. (6 sc)

Round 2: 1 ch, 2 dc into each st, sl st into first dc to join. (12 sc)

Fasten off, leaving a 30cm (12in) tail.

Finishing

Use tail end of yarn to sew the ears and eyes into place, using the photograph as a guide.

2

ONE-EYED ALIENS

HELPFUL TIP

Make sure you sew the antennae on very firmly and weave in the ends thoroughly to help secure them.

These spunky cyclops aliens will warm your baby's feet and bring a smile to all who see them. A simple project to stitch up and rocket your baby's wardrobe out of this world.

BEFORE YOU BEGIN

SKILL LEVEL
1

YOU WILL NEED
Debbie Bliss Baby Cashmerino
50g (1.75oz); 125m (136yds);
33% microfibre/55% wool/
12% cashmere
1 in Apple (02) = MC
Small amount of white yarn = CC1
Small amount of Royal (70) = CC2

Hook
3.5mm (US E/4)
Adjust hook size if necessary to achieve correct tension

Notions
Black embroidery thread
Stitch marker
Yarn needle

TENSION
10 sts and 10 rows in dc to measure 5cm (2in)

SIZES
0–6 months, sole length 9cm (3½in)
6–12 months, sole length 10cm (4in)

Note: Instructions are given for the smallest size first; the larger size is given in square brackets [ ]

STITCHES AND SKILLS
See Crochet Basics (pages 134–142)

Sole 1
Working in rows
Working in rounds
Working into front and back loops
Crab stitch

To Make the Booties

(make 2)

Sole

Using MC, make Sole 1.

Do not fasten off, but cont with upper.

Upper

Using MC.

Round 1: 1 ch, miss st at base of 1 ch, 1 dc blo into each of next 45[49] sts, sl st into first dc to join.

Rounds 2–3: Working under both loops of every st, rep Round 1.

Round 4: 1 ch, 1 dc into each of next 6 sts, *miss next st, 1 dc into next st; rep from * 8[10] more times, 1 dc into each of next 21 sts, sl st into first dc to join.

ONE-EYED ALIENS

Round 5: 1 ch, 1 dc into each of next 4 sts, *miss next st, 1 dc into next st; rep from * 5[6] more times, 1 dc into each of next 20 sts, sl st into first dc to join.

Round 6: 1 ch, 1 dc into each of next 30[31] sts, sl st into first dc to join.

Round 7: 1 ch, 1 dc into each of next 3 sts, *miss next st, 1 sc into next st; rep from * 4 more times, 1 dc into each of next 17[18] sts, sl st into first dc to join.

Round 8: 1 ch, 1 dc into each of next 25[26] sts, sl st into first dc to join.

Rounds 9–13: Rep Round 8 5 more times.

Round 14: 1 ch, work 1 crab st into each st, sl st into first crab st to join. Fasten off.

Antennae

(make 2 per bootie)

Using MC.
Row 1: Make 6 ch, 2 dc into 2nd ch from hook, 1 sl st into each rem ch. (6 sts)

Fasten off.

Eyeball

Using CC1.
Foundation ring: Make 3 ch, sl st into first ch to join.

Round 1: 1 ch, 8 dc into the ring. (8 sts)

Cont to work in a spiral.

Round 2: 2 dc into each st, sl st into first dc to join. (16 sts)

Fasten off, leaving a tail.

Iris

Using CC2.
Foundation ring: Make 3 ch, sl st into first ch to join.

Round 1: 1 ch, 8 dc into the ring, sl st into first dc to join. (8 sts)

Fasten off, leaving a tail.

Finishing

Sew each blue iris to the centre of each white eyeball, using the tail end of yarn from the blue iris. Sew a small dot in the centre of each iris using black embroidery thread. Sew one eye on to the front of each boot using the tail end of yarn from the white eyeball. Sew a smile underneath the eye using black embroidery thread and backstitch. Weave ends into WS and trim. Sew the antennae to each side of the eye, using the photograph as a guide.

3
MONSTER
CLAWS

Transform those sweet baby toes into funky monster claws with these colourful booties. The booties are worked in rounds with snaggly nails attached for truly terrible toes.

BEFORE YOU BEGIN

SKILL LEVEL
3

YOU WILL NEED
Sirdar Snuggly DK 50g (1.75oz); 165m (179yds); 55% nylon/ 45% acrylic
1 in Dusty Blue (449) = MC
Small amount of Gumdrop (444) = CC1

Hook
3.25mm (US D/3)
Adjust hook size if necessary to achieve correct tension

Notions
Stitch marker
Yarn needle

TENSION
10 sts and 12 rows in dc to measure 5cm (2in)

SIZES
0–6 months, sole length 9cm (3½in)
6–12 months, sole length 10cm (4in)

Note: Instructions are given for the smallest size first; the larger size is given in square brackets [ ]

STITCHES AND SKILLS
See Crochet Basics (pages 134–142)
Working in rows
Working in rounds
Working into back loops
Magic loop
dc2tog

NOTES
MC yarn used in photographs is Bluebell Mix (354), discontinued.
Pattern is worked toe-up, in rounds. Unless stated do not turn at the end of a round.
Sl st into first dc to join each round.
Initial 1 ch does not count as st.
Make first st(s) in same space as 1 ch.

To Make the Booties

(make 2)

Toes

(make 4 per bootie)

Work slightly tighter sts for toes only.

Using MC.
Round 1: 8 dc into a magic loop, pull magic loop to close shut, sl st into first dc to join. (8 sts)

Rounds 2–3: 1 ch, 1 dc into each st, sl st into first dc to join.

Fasten off. Make 3 more toes but do not fasten off the 4th toe.

Join toes: With hook in working loop of 4th toe *insert hook into the next st of a fastened off toe and make 1 dc into this st and 1 dc into each of next 3 sts, rep from * with rem toes. Cont to work 1 dc into rem 4 sts of each toe, sl st into first dc to join and place marker in last st to mark end of Round. (32 sts). Cont with foot.

Foot
Work into blo.

Round 1: 1 ch, 1 dc into every st. (32 sts)

Round 2: 1 ch, 1 dc into next st, *1 dc into each of next 2 sts, dc2tog, rep from * 6 more times, 1 dc into each of next 3 sts. (25 sts)

Round 3: 1 ch, 1 dc into each st.

Rep Round 3 6[7] more times or until piece measures 6cm (2½in) [7cm (3in)].

Next Round: 1 ch, 1 dc into each st but do not join round. Cont with heel.

Heel
Work in rows.

Row 1: 1 ch, 1 dc blo into each of next 13 sts, leave rem sts unworked, turn. (13 sts)

Row 2: 1 ch, 1 dc (working under both loops) into each of next 18 sts, leave rem sts unworked, turn. (18 sts)

Row 3: 1 ch, 1 dc into each st, turn.

Rep last row 5[6] more times.

Row 9[10]: 1 ch, 1 dc into each of next 4 sts, dc2tog, 1 dc into each of next 2 sts, dc2tog, 1 dc into each of next 2 sts, dc2tog, 1 dc into each of next 4 sts, turn.

Row 10[11]: 1 ch, 1 dc into each of next 2 sts, dc2tog, 1 dc into each of next 2 sts, dc2tog, 1 dc into each of next 2 sts, dc2tog, 1 dc into each of next 3 sts, turn.

Row 11[12]: 1 ch, 1 dc into each of next 3 sts, *dc2tog, rep from * twice more, 1 dc into each of next 3 sts, sl st into first dc to join.

Ankle
Work in rounds.

Using MC.
Round 1: 1 ch, evenly work 10[11] dc along the side rows, 1 dc into each rem st from Round 1 of heel, evenly work 10[11] dc along the side rows. (27[29]sts)

Round 2: 1 ch, 1 dc blo into each st.

Rep last round 3[4] more times. Fasten off.

Nails
(make 4 per foot)

Using CC1.
Row 1: Make 4 ch, 1 dc into 2nd ch from hook, 1 htr into next ch, 1 tr into last ch. Fasten off and leave tail to sew on to toes.

Finishing
Weave ends into WS. Stitch each nail on to each toe. Sew back seam.

4 LITTLE MONSTER BOOTIES

Full of personality with their mismatched eyes and cute tail, these stripy shoes will delight anyone who spots your little monster. The toe is worked in the round and the soles and sides are worked flat.

BEFORE YOU BEGIN

SKILL LEVEL
2

YOU WILL NEED
Debbie Bliss Rialto DK 50g (1.75oz); 105m (115yds); 100% merino wool
1 in Pool (70) = MC
Small amount of Sky (60) = CC1
Small amount of white yarn = CC2

Hook
3.5mm (US E/4)
Adjust hook size if necessary to achieve correct tension

Notions
Black embroidery thread
Stitch marker
Yarn needle

TENSION
10 sts and 10 rows in dc to measure 5cm (2in)

SIZES
0–6 months, sole length 9cm (3½in)
6–12 months, sole length 10cm (4in)

Note: Instructions are given for the smallest size first; the larger size is given in square brackets [ ]

STITCHES AND SKILLS
See Crochet Basics (pages 134–142)

Working in rows
Working in rounds
dc2tog

To Make the Booties

(make 2)

Toe

Using MC.
Foundation ring: Make 4 ch, sl st into first ch to join.

Round 1: 1 ch, 8 dc into the ring, sl st into first dc to join. (8 sts)

Cont to work in a spiral without joining rounds.

Round 2: 2 dc into each st. (16 sts)

HELPFUL TIP

For an eye-catching variation, choose contrasting colours for the monster's stripes.

Round 3: Change to CC1, *1 dc into next st, 2 dc into next st, rep from * to end. (24 sts)

Round 4: 1 dc into each st. (24 sts)

Round 5: Change to MC, 1 dc into each st. (24 sts)

Round 6: *1 dc into each of next 2 sts, 2 dc into next st, rep from * to end. (32 sts)

Rounds 7–8: Change to CC1, 1 dc into each st. (32 sts)

Round 9: Change to MC, 1 dc into each st. (32 sts)

Round 10: 1 dc into each st, place marker. (32 sts)

Fasten off. You will now work in rows for the sides and the sole.

Sides and Sole

Row 1: Miss 20 sts, using CC1 sl st into 21st st, 1 ch, 1 dc into st at base of 1 ch, 1 dc into each of next 23 sts, turn. (24 sts)

Row 2: 1 ch, 1 dc into each st, turn (24 sts)

Keeping stripes correct, changing colour every 2 rows, rep Row 2 10[12] times.

Fasten off.

Heel

Join CC1[MC] into 8th st from the right-hand heel edge.

Row 1: 1 ch, 1 dc into st at the base of 1 ch, 1 dc into each of next 7 sts, turn. (8 sts)

Row 2: Rep Row 1, turn.

Keeping stripes correct, changing colour every two rows.

Rows 3–8: Rep Row 1 6 times. Fasten off.

With WS facing you (turn the bootie inside out) and right sides together, place the heel and side edges together. Working through both layers, join two seams together with a sl st. Fasten off and weave ends into WS.

Next Round: Join MC to the corner of left-hand toe edge and Row 1 of the shoe side, work 10[12] dc evenly along the side, dc2tog across the corner of the side and the heel, 4 dc evenly across the top of the heel, dc2tog across the corner of the side and the heel, and work 10[12] dc evenly along the right-hand side edge. Fasten off and weave ends into WS.

Spikes

You will work the spikes into the last row at the toe edge. Work with toe of shoe facing.

Row 1: Join MC with a sl st into first dc of toe edge, *(2 htr, 2 ch, 2 htr) into next st, sl st into each of next 2 sts; rep from * twice more.

Fasten off and weave ends into WS.

Tail

Using MC.
Row 1: Make 7 ch, 1 dc into 2nd ch from hook, 1 dc into each rem ch. (6 sts)

Fasten off leaving a long tail of yarn.

Attach CC1 to first ch with a sl st, 1 ch, 3 dc into same ch. Fasten off.

Eyes

(make 2 per bootie)

Using CC2.
Foundation ring: Make 3 ch, sl st into first ch to join.

Round 1: 1 ch, 8 dc into the ring, sl st into first dc to join. Fasten off, leaving a tail.

Finishing

Sew the eye to the toe using the tail of yarn. Sew a small dot in the centre of the eye using black embroidery thread. Sew a cross for another eye using CC2 yarn. Sew a smile underneath the eye using backstitch and black embroidery thread. Sew a small triangle beneath the mouth for a tooth using CC2 yarn. Sew the tail of the monster in the centre of the heel using the tail of yarn. Weave ends into WS.

HELPFUL TIP

Why not make these booties as twins – one with a smiley face and one with a frown?

5

BEEPBOT BOOTIES

Beep Beep! These friendly robot booties make perfect companions for those active little feet. The double-sided head is sewn together and has appliqué eyes and ears.

BEFORE YOU BEGIN

SKILL LEVEL
2

YOU WILL NEED
Debbie Bliss Mia 50g (1.75oz); 100m (109yds); 50% cotton/50% wool
1 in Robin Egg (05) = MC
Small amount of Cinnamon (13) = CC1
Small amount of white yarn = CC2

Hook
3.5mm (US E/4)
Adjust hook size if necessary to achieve correct tension

Notions
Black embroidery thread
Stitch marker
Yarn needle

TENSION
10 sts and 10 rows in dc to measure 5cm (2in)

SIZES
0–6 months, sole length 9cm (3½in)
6–12 months, sole length 10cm (4in)

Note: Instructions are given for the smallest size first; the larger size is given in square brackets [ ]

STITCHES AND SKILLS
See Crochet Basics (pages 134–142)

Sole 1
Working in rows
Working in rounds
tr2tog
Crab stitch

To Make the Booties

(make 2)

Sole

Using MC, make Sole 1.

Do not fasten off, but cont with upper.

Upper

Using MC.

Round 1: 1 ch, miss st at base of 1 ch, 1 dc blo in each of next 45[49] sts, sl st into first dc to join.

For larger size only, work decrease round as follows: working under both loops, 1 ch, 1 dc into each of next 11 sts, miss next 2 sts, 1 tr into next 9 sts, miss next 2 sts, 1 dc into each of next 25 sts, sl st into first dc to join. (45 sts)

Cont for both sizes, working under both loops:

Round 2: 1 ch, 1 dc into each of next 9 sts, miss next 2 sts, 1 tr into each of next 9 sts, miss next 2 sts, 1 dc into each of next 23 sts, sl st into first dc to join. (41 sts)

Round 3: 1 ch, 1 dc into each of next 7 sts, miss next 2 sts, 1 tr into each of next 9 sts, miss next 2 sts, 1 dc into each of next 21 sts, sl st into first dc to join. (37 sts)

Round 4: 1 ch, 1 dc into each of next 5 sts, miss next 2 sts, 1 tr into each of next 9 sts, miss next 2 sts, 1 dc into each of next 19 sts, sl st into first dc to join. (33 sts)

Round 5: 1 ch, 1 dc into each of next 3 sts, miss next 2 sts, 1 tr into each of next 9 sts, miss next 2 sts, 1 dc into each of next 17 sts, sl st into first dc to join. (29 sts)

Round 6: 3 ch (counts as 1 tr), 1 tr into each of next 3 sts, tr2tog 5 times, 1 tr into each of next 16 sts, sl st into 3rd of first 3 ch to join. (24 sts)

Round 7: Join in CC1, 1 ch, work 1 crab st into each st to end, sl st into first crab st to join. Fasten off.

Head – Front and Back

(make 2 per bootie)

Using MC.
Row 1: Make 8 ch, 1 dc into 2nd ch from hook, 1 dc into each rem ch, turn. (7 sts)

Row 2: 1 ch, 1 dc in each st, turn.

Rows 3–16: Rep Row 2 14 more times. Fasten off.

Head – Sides

(make 4 per bootie)

Using MC.
Row 1: Make 5 ch, 1 dc into 2nd ch from hook, 1 dc into each rem ch, turn. (4 sts)

Row 2: 1 ch, 1 dc into each st, turn.

Rows 3–6: Rep Row 2 4 more times. Fasten off.

Eyes

(make 2 per bootie)

Using CC2.
Foundation ring: Make 3 ch, sl st into 3rd ch from hook to join.

Round 1: 1 ch, 8 dc into the ring, sl st into first dc to join. (8 sts)

Fasten off leaving a tail.

Ears

(make 2 per bootie)

Using CC1.
Foundation ring: Make 3 ch, sl st into 3rd ch from hook to join.

Round 1: 1 ch, 8 dc into the ring, sl st into first dc to join. (8 sts)

Fasten off leaving a tail.

Arms

(make 2 per bootie)

Using MC.

Row 1: Make 7 ch, 1 dc into 2nd ch from hook, 1 dc into each rem ch, turn. (6 sts)

Row 2: 1 ch, 1 dc into each st, turn.

Row 3: Rep row 2. Fasten off.

With CC1 attach yarn with a sl st to the short end (row end) of the arm, 3 ch, sl st into st at opposite end, turn, 4 dc into 3 ch sp.

Fasten off and weave ends into WS.

Finishing

Using the photograph as a guide, sew the arms to the top of the bootie, just below Round 7.

Sew each side of the head to the front and back of the head, working up the front of the face along the top of the head and then down the back. Sew an ear in the middle of each side of the head using a tail of yarn. Sew the white eyes on to the front of the head. Sew a small stitch in the centre of the eyes for a pupil using black embroidery thread. Sew the mouth using backstitch and black embroidery thread. Once you have completed the features of the head, fold the head in half and using MC sew the base of the head together. Sew the head in place at the top of the bootie just between Rounds 6 and 7.

HELPFUL TIP

For extra pizzazz why not make these booties in a silver lurex yarn to dress them up for a special party?

6

FEISTY DRAGONS

Add some fire to your baby's feet with these green dragon booties. Perfect for keeping little feet warm and toasty.

BEFORE YOU BEGIN

SKILL LEVEL

2

YOU WILL NEED

Debbie Bliss Baby Cashmerino
50g (1.75oz); 125m (136yds);
33% microfibre/55% wool/
12% cashmere
2 in Apple (02) = MC
Small amount of black yarn = CC1
Small amount of Ruby (700) = CC2
1 in Forest (77) = CC3

Hook

3.5mm (US E/4)
4.5mm (US 7)
Adjust hook size if necessary to achieve correct tension

Notions

Polyester fibre filling
(small amount for stuffing)
Stitch marker
Yarn needle

TENSION

9 sts and 6 rows in htr to measure 5cm (2in) using two strands of MC

SIZES

0–6 months, sole length 10cm (4in)
6–12 months, sole length 11cm (4¼in)
Note: Instructions are given for the smallest size first; the larger size is given in square brackets [ ]

STITCHES AND SKILLS

See Crochet Basics
(pages 134–142)

Working in rows
Working in rounds
Magic loop
dc2tog

NOTES

CC3 yarn used in photographs is Basil (61), discontinued.
Make sure that you join a round into the first htr or top of 1 ch/2 ch and start a new round by crocheting into the next st, not into the st where you joined the round. The last st of a round is the 'sl st into first htr/1 ch/2 ch to join.'

To Make the Booties

(make 2)

Sole

Using MC (two strands) and larger hook.

Round 1: Make 11[13] ch, 1 htr into 3rd ch from hook, 1 htr into each of next 7[9] sts, 6 htr into last ch, working on opposite side, 1 htr into next 7[9] sts, 5 htr into last ch, sl st into first htr to join. (26 [30] sts)

HELPFUL TIP

The sole and upper are worked with two strands of MC held together. If you are using DK yarn then use a single strand to achieve the same sole length.

Round 2: 1 ch, 1 htr into each of next 8[10] sts, 2 htr into each of next 5 sts, 1 htr into next 8[10] sts, 2 htr into each of next 5 sts, sl st into first htr to join. (36[40] sts)

Round 3: 1 ch, 1 htr into each of next 8[10] sts, *2 htr into next st, 1 htr into next st; rep from * 4 more times, 1 htr into next 8[10] sts, *2 htr into next st, 1 htr into next st; rep from * 4 more times, sl st into first htr to join. (46[50] sts)

Upper

Cont with MC (two strands) and larger hook.
Round 1: 1 ch, 1 htr blo into each of next 46[50] sts, sl st into 1 ch to join. (46[50] sts)

Round 2: Rep Round 1.

Round 3: 1 ch, 1 dc into each of next 8 sts, *dc2tog over the next 2 sts; rep from * 9[11] more times, 1 dc into each of next 18 sts, sl st into 1 ch to join. (36[38] sts)

Round 4: 1 ch, 1 htr into each of next 36[38] sts, sl st into 1 ch to join. (36[38] sts)

Round 5: 1 ch, 1 dc into each of next 10 sts, *dc2tog over next 2 sts ; rep from * 4[5] more times, 1 dc into each of next 16 sts, sl st into 1 ch to join. (31[32] sts)

Round 6: 1 ch, 1 htr into each of next 31[32] sts, sl st into 1 ch to join. (31[32] sts)

Round 7: 1 ch, 1 dc into each of next 10 sts, *dc2tog over the next 2 sts; rep from * twice more, 1 dc into each of next 15[16] sts, sl st into 1 ch to join. (28[29] sts)

Round 8: 1 ch, 1 htr into each of next 28[29] sts, sl st into ch 1 to join. (28[29] sts)

Round 9: 1 ch, 1 htr into each of next 28[29] sts, sl st into ch 1 to join. (28[29] sts)

Fasten off leaving a tail of approx 15cm (6in). Make a double knot with the yarn, weave ends into WS and trim.

Ears

(make 2 per bootie)

Using MC (single strand) and smaller hook.
Round 1: Make 2 ch, work 4 dc into 2nd ch from hook. Cont to work in a spiral.

Round 2: *2 dc into next st, 1 dc into next st; rep from * to end. (6 sts)

Round 3: *2 dc into next st, 1 dc into each of next 2 sts; rep from * to end. (8 sts)

Round 4: *2 dc into next st, 1 dc into each of next 3 sts; rep from * to end. (10 sts)

Round 5: *2 dc into next st, 1 dc into each of next 4 sts; rep from * to end. (12 sts)

Round 6: *2 dc into next st, 1 dc into each of next 5 sts; rep from * to end. (14 sts)

Round 7: *2 dc into next st, 1 dc into each of next 6 sts; rep from * to end. (16 sts)

Round 8: *Dc2tog, 1 dc into each of next 6 sts; rep from * to end. (14 sts)

Round 9: *Dc2tog, 1 dc into each of next 5 sts; rep from * to end. (12 sts)

Round 10: *Dc2tog, 1 dc into each of next 4 sts; rep from * to end. (10 sts)

Round 11: 1 dc into each of next 5 sts.

Fasten off, leaving a tail of approx 30cm (12in) and using a yarn needle, sew the ears to each side of top of the boot at Round 8. Weave ends into WS.

Eyes

(make 2 per bootie)

Using CC1 (single strand) and smaller hook.
Round 1: Make 2 ch, work 6 dc into 2nd ch from hook, sl st into first dc to join. (6 sts)

Fasten off, leaving a tail of approx 20cm (8in). Using yarn needle, sew the eyes to the front of the bootie at Rounds 5–6. Weave yarn ends into WS of bootie.

Tongue

(make 1 per bootie)

Using CC2 (single strand) and smaller hook.
Row 1: Make 8 ch, 1 dc into 2nd ch from hook, 1 dc into next st, 3 ch, 1 dc into 2nd ch from hook, 1 dc into next st, 1 dc into next 5 sts to end. (7 sts)

Fasten off, leaving a tail of approx 20cm (8in) and with a yarn needle, sew the tongue to the bottom front of the boot at Round 1. Ensure that the tongue is placed in the centre of the bootie's toe cap. Weave ends into WS.

Spikes

(make 3 per bootie)

Using CC3 (single strand) and smaller hook.
Round 1: Make 5 ch, 1 dc into 2nd ch from hook, 1 dc into each rem ch. (4 sts)

Round 2: *2 dc into next st, 1 dc into next st; rep from * to end. (6 sts)

Round 3: *2 dc into next st, 1 dc into each of next 2 sts; rep from * to end. (8 sts)

Round 4: 1 dc into each st. (8 sts)

Round 5: Rep Round 4.

Fasten off, leaving a tail of approx 30cm (12in). Stuff each spike with a small amount of polyester fibre filling and use a yarn needle to sew the spikes down the back of the booties. Make sure that the spikes are evenly spaced and centred in between the ears and eyes (lining up with the attached tongue in the front). Weave ends into WS of bootie.

7
DINO
STOMPERS

Dinosaurs may be extinct but you can bring them back to life with these unique booties. Get creative and stitch up extra pairs in your favourite colour combinations.

BEFORE YOU BEGIN

SKILL LEVEL
2

YOU WILL NEED
Debbie Bliss Mia 50g (1.75oz); 100m (109yds); 50% cotton/ 5% wool
1 in Aqua (17) = MC
1 in Corn (14) = CC1
Small amount of DK weight yarn in black = CC2

Hook
4mm (US 6)
Adjust hook size if necessary to achieve correct tension

Notions
Stitch marker
Yarn needle

TENSION
20 sts and 22 rows in dc to measure 10cm (4in)

SIZES
0–6 months, sole length 9cm (3½in)
6–12 months, sole length 10cm (4in)

Note: Instructions are given for the smallest size first; the larger size is given in square brackets [ ]

STITCHES AND SKILLS
See Crochet Basics (pages 134–142)

Working in rows
Working in rounds
Working into front and back loops
Magic loop
dc2tog
dc3tog
Shell stitch

To Make the Booties

(make 2)

Toe

Using MC.

Round 1: Make 3[4] ch, 2 dc into 2nd ch from hook, 1 dc into next 0[1] ch, 4 dc into last chain. Working into opposite side of the ch, 1 dc into next 0[1] ch, 2 dc into ch that already contains first 2 dc. (8[10] sts)

Round 2: 2 dc into first st, 1 dc into each of next 2[3] sts, 2 dc into each of next 2 sts, 1 dc into each of next 2[3] sts, 2 dc into last st. (12[14] sts)

Round 3: 2 dc into first st, 1 dc into each of next 4[5] sts, 2 dc into each of next 2 sts, 1 dc into each of next 4[5] sts, 2 dc into last st. (16[18] sts)

Round 4: 2 dc into each of first 2 sts, 1 dc into each of next 6[7] sts, 2 dc into each of next 2 sts, 1 dc into each of next 6[7] sts. (20[22] sts)

Round 5: 1 dc into each st. (20[22] sts)

Rounds 6–10[11]: Rep Round 5 5[6] more times. (20[22] sts)

Body

Row 1: 1 dc into each of next 16[17] sts, dc2tog, 1 ch, turn, leaving rem 2[3] sts unworked. (17[18] sts)

Mark the side of Row 1 by slipping a stitch marker around the 1 ch.

Row 2: Dc2tog, 1 dc into each of the next 14[16] sts, dc2tog, leaving rem st unworked, 1 ch, turn. (16[18] sts)

Row 3: Dc2tog, 1 dc into each of next 14[16] sts, 1 ch, turn. (15[17] sts)

Row 4: 1 dc into each st, 1 ch, turn. (15[17] sts)

Row 5–11[13]: Rep Row 4 7[9] more times. (15[17] sts)

Mark last st of row 11 if you are making the smaller size.

For larger size only: Row 14: Dc2tog, 1 dc into each of next 13 sts, dc2tog, 1 ch, turn. (15 sts)

Mark last st of Row 14 if you are making the larger size.

Tail

Row 1: Dc2tog, 1 dc into each of next 11 sts, dc2tog, 1 ch, turn. (13 sts)

Row 2: Dc2tog, 1 dc into each of next 9 sts, dc2tog, 1 ch, turn. (11 sts)

Row 3: Dc2tog, 1 dc into each of next 7 sts, dc2tog, 1 ch, turn. (9 sts)

Row 4: 1 dc into each st, 1 ch, turn. (9 sts)

Row 5: Dc2tog, 1 dc into each of next 5 sts, dc2tog, 1 ch, turn. (7 sts)

Row 6: 1 dc into each st, 1 ch, turn. (7 sts)

Row 7: Dc2tog, 1 dc into each of next 3 sts, dc2tog, 1 ch, turn. (5 sts)

Row 8: 1 dc into each st, 1 ch, turn. (5 sts)

Row 9: Dc2tog, 1 dc into next st, dc2tog, 1 ch, turn. (3 sts)

Row 10: 1 dc into each st, 1 ch, turn. (3 sts)

Row 11: Dc3tog, 1 ch. (1 st)

Fold bootie in half with RS facing out. Working through both layers, close the tail by working a dc into each row up the side for a total of 10 dc. Sl st into the next row, which should be the marked Row 11 [14] of the body, 1 ch and fasten off. Remove stitch marker.

Edging Rows

You will now work around the opening of the bootie, starting in the first (marked) row on the right and ending on the left. You will be working with the inside of the bootie facing you.

Row 1: Join MC by making a sl st in the first (marked) row on the right, work 9[11] dc, working into each row of the right side. Cont around, work 9 [11] dc working into each row of the opposite side, sl st into the next row, 1 ch, turn. (18[22] sts)

Row 2: Miss the sl st, *1 htr into next st, 2 tr into next st, 2 dtr into next st, 1 dtr into each of next 2 sts, 2 dtr into next st, 2 tr into next st, 1 htr into next st*, 1 dc into each of next 2 sts, [2 dc into the next 2 sts, 1 dc into each of next 2 sts]; rep from * to *, sl st into the next row of the bootie, which will already contain a sl st. Fasten off and weave ends into WS. (26[32] sts)

Adding Spikes

Using CC1.

With RS facing, join yarn with a sl st into first st of edging Row 2. Work 4[5] shells over next 12[15] sts, which brings you to the tail, sl st into flo of first dc of tail, work 3 shells over the rem 9 sts, working into flo, 1 ch, turn. You will now work into the rem back loop of each st, sl st into rem loop of same st, work 3 shells over the rem 9 sts, working into flo. This will bring you back to the body. Working through both loops again, sl st in the next available st of the body (which will be a dc), work 4[5] shells over the next 12[15] sts, fasten off and weave ends into WS.

Horn

Using CC1.

Round 1: 3 dc into a magic loop, pull magic loop to close shut. (3 sc)

Cont to work in a spiral.

Round 2: 1 dc into next st, 2 dc into each of next 2 sts. (5 sts)

Round 3: 1 dc into each of next 3 sts, 2 dc into each of next 2 sts. (7 sts)

Round 4: 1 dc into each of next 3 sts, *2 dc into next st, 1 dc into next st; rep from * once more. (9 sts)

Round 5: 1 dc into each of next 3 sts, *2 dc into next st, 1 dc into each of next 2 sts; rep from * once more, sl st into next st, 1 ch and fasten off, leaving a 15cm (6in) tail. (11 sts)

Use the initial tail of yarn to stuff the horn. Use the end tail of yarn to attach the horn to the bootie, placing it in the middle and over Rounds 1–5 of the bootie.

Legs

(make 4 per bootie)

Using MC.

Round 1: 6 dc into a magic loop, pull magic loop to close shut. (6 sc)

Cont to work in a spiral.

Round 2: 1 dc into each st. (6 sts)

Round 3: Rep Round 2, 1 ch and fasten off, leaving a 15cm (6in) tail. (6 sts)

Finishing

Fold the bootie flat so that the fold runs along the bottom of the dinosaur's body. Attach the legs so that the closed ends (feet) line up with the bottom fold of the bootie. Attach the legs in line with the first and last spikes on the body (not the tail). To attach each leg, fold it in half and use the tail end of the yarn to sew the top shut. Sew the top of the leg to the body with a couple of back sts. Attach the middle of the leg to the body by catching it with a couple of back sts too. If you do not attach the legs at both the top and the middle, they will stick out like flippers. Next, embroider the eyes as follows: fold the bootie flat so that the horn is facing you. Mark the position of the eyes on Round 10 of the bootie, and in line with the outside edges of the horn. Sew a couple of back sts for each eye, using CC2.

8 MAGICAL UNICORNS

Bring mythical and magical unicorns to life with these adorable booties. Try using multi-coloured yarn in place of the pink to give them some extra sparkle.

BEFORE YOU BEGIN

SKILL LEVEL
2

YOU WILL NEED
Debbie Bliss Baby Cashmerino
50g (1.75oz); 125m (136yds); 33% microfibre/55% wool/
12% cashmere
1 in Ecru 101 = MC
1 in Candy Pink (06) = CC1
Small amount of yellow yarn = CC2
Small amount of beige yarn = CC3
Small amount of black yarn = CC4

Hook
3.5mm (US E/4)
4.5mm (US 7)
Adjust hook size if necessary to achieve correct tension

Notions
Stitch marker
Yarn needle

TENSION
9 sts and 10 rows in dc to measure 5cm (2in) using two strands of MC

SIZES
0–6 months, sole length 10cm (4in)
6–12 months, sole length 11cm (4½in)

Note: Instructions are given for the smallest size first; the larger size is given in square brackets [ ]

STITCHES AND SKILLS
See Crochet Basics (pages 134–142)

Working in rows
Working in rounds
Working into back loops
dc2tog
Loop stitch

NOTES
Make sure that you join a round into the first htr/1 ch/2 ch and start a new round by crocheting into the next st, not into the st where you joined the round. The last stitch of a round is the 'sl st into first htr/1 ch/2 ch to join.'

To Make the Booties

(make 2)

Sole

Using CC1 (two strands) and larger hook.
Round 1: Make 11[13] ch, 1 htr into 3rd ch from hook, 1 htr into each of next 7[9] sts, 6 htr into last ch, working on opposite side, 1 htr into each of next 7[9] sts, 5 htr into last ch, sl st into first htr to join. (26[30] sts)

HELPFUL TIP

The sole and upper are worked using two strands of CC1 or MC held together. If you are using DK yarn then use a single strand to achieve the same sole length.

Round 2: 1 ch, 1 htr into each of next 8[10] sts, 2 htr into each of next 5 sts, 1 htr into each of next 8[10] sts, 2 htr into each of next 5 sts, sl st into first htr to join. (36[40] sts)

Round 3: 1 ch, 1 htr into each of next 8[10] sts, *2 htr into next st, 1 htr into next st; rep from * 4 more times, 1 htr into each of next 8[10] sts, *2 htr into next st, 1 htr into next st; rep from * 4 more times, sl st into first htr to join, changing to MC (two strands) during sl st. (46[50] sts)

Upper

Cont using MC (two strands) and larger hook.
Round 1: 2 ch, 1 tr blo into each of next 46[50] sts, sl st into top ch of 2 ch to join. (46 [50] sts)

Round 2: 1 ch, 1 dc (working under both loops) into each of next 46 [50] sts, sl st into 1 ch to join. (46[50] sts)

Round 3: 1 ch, 1 dc into each of next 6 sts, *dc2tog; rep from * 9[11] more times, 1 dc into each of next 20 sts, sl st into 1 ch to join. (36[38] sts)

Round 4: 1 ch, 1 dc into each of next 36[38] sts, sl st into 1 ch to join. (36[38] sts)

Round 5: 1 ch, 1 dc into each of next 6 sts, *dc2tog; rep from * 4[5] more times, 1 dc into each of next 20 sts, sl st into 1 ch to join. (31[32] sts)

Fasten off, leaving a tail of approx 15cm (6in) and weave ends into WS.

Face

Using MC (single strand) and smaller hook.
Round 1: Make 2 ch, 6 dc into 2nd ch from hook. (6 sts)

Round 2: 2 dc into each st. (12 sts)

Round 3: 2 dc into each st. (24 sts)

Round 4: 1 dc into each st. (24 sts)

Round 5: * 2 dc into next st, 1 dc into each of next 3 sts; rep from * 5 more times. (30 sts)

Round 6: 1 dc into each of next 3 sts, 2 dc into each of next 2 sts, 1 dc into each of next 5 sts, 2 dc into each of next 2 sts, 1 dc into each of next 18 sts. (34 sts)

Fasten off leaving a tail end of approx 45cm (18in) to attach the finished unicorn face to the front of the bootie. The face will be sewn to the bootie after the ears, mane and horn have been attached.

Ears

(make 2 per bootie)

Using MC (single strand) and smaller hook.
Round 1: Make 2 ch, 4 dc into 2nd ch from hook.(4 sts)

Round 2: *2 dc into next st, 1 dc into next st; rep from * to end. (6 sts)

Round 3: *2 dc into next st, 1 dc into each of next 2 sts; rep from * to end. (8 sts)

Round 4: 1 dc into each st. (8 sts)

Round 5: 1 dc into each st. (8 sts)

HELPFUL TIP

The '2 dc in next 2 sts' sections of the face (Round 6) are where the ears are to be attached.

Fasten off, leaving a tail of approx 30cm (12in). Sew the ears to each side of top of the head (see tip page 41 for ear location) leaving 6 sts in between the ears. Secure with a double knot and weave in the yarn end into the WS of face.

Mane

Using CC1 (single strand) and smaller hook. Turn the face piece around and work from the WS. The mane will be worked into the 6 sts in between the attached ears. Place the crochet hook into the first stitch next to the ear and attach the yarn. Make a loop st into each of the 6 sts in between the ears. (6 loops). Fasten off and weave in both yarn ends with a yarn needle.

Horn

Using CC2 (single strand) and smaller hook.
Round 1: Make 2 ch, 4 dc into 2nd ch from hook. (4 sts)

Round 2: *2 dc into next st, 1 dc into next st; rep from * to end. (6 sts)

Rounds 3–5: 1 dc into each st. (6 sts)

Fasten off, leaving a tail end of 20cm (8in). Using a yarn needle, sew the horn to the top of the unicorn face underneath the mane. Secure with a double knot and weave ends into WS. Using CC4 and a yarn needle, sew eyes on to the face underneath the horn making sure to leave space for the nose to be sewn on later. Ensure that the eyes are secured with a double knot.

Nose

Using CC3 (single strand) and smaller hook.
Row 1: Make 11 ch, 1 dc into 2nd ch from hook, 1 dc into each rem ch. Turn. (10 sts)

Row 2: 1 ch, 2 dc into first st, 1 dc into each of next 8 sts, 2 dc into last st. Turn. (12 sts)

Row 3: 1 ch, 2 dc into first st, 1 dc into each of next 10 sts, 2 dc into last st. Turn. (14 sts)

Rows 4–5: 1 ch, 1 dc into each st. Turn. (14 sts)

Next, work a dc border of approx 35 sts all around nose piece, sl st into first dc to join. Fasten off, leaving a tail of approx 60cm (24in) to attach nose to the front of the bootie. Using CC4 and a yarn needle, sew nostrils on to the nose towards the crescent part of the nose. Make sure that the nostrils are secured with a double knot.

Finishing

Place the face over the front of the bootie so that the ears are aligned with the edge of the bootie (the mane and horn will protrude over the edge). Using a yarn needle and the rem yarn from the face, sew the face to the front of the booties. Fasten off, secure with a double knot and weave ends into WS. Place the nose over the attached face so that the crescent section aligns with the pink sole of the bootie and the straight edge of the nose is under the eyes. With a yarn needle and the rem yarn from the nose, sew the nose to the front of the bootie. Fasten off, secure with a double knot and weave ends into WS.

WILD ANIMALS

9
PLAYFUL
PANDAS

These adorable panda booties will look great with a plain white onesie or sleepsuit. Your baby will love reaching for the sweet faces on these shoes, guaranteed to become favourite companions.

BEFORE YOU BEGIN

SKILL LEVEL
1

YOU WILL NEED
Debbie Bliss Rialto DK 50g (1.75oz); 105m (115yds) 100% merino wool
1 in Black (03) = MC
25g (1oz) DK weight yarn in white = CC1

Hook
3.5mm (US E/4)
Adjust hook size if necessary to achieve correct tension

Notions
Black embroidery thread
Blue embroidery thread
Stitch marker
Yarn needle

TENSION
10 sts and 10 rows in dc to measure 5cm (2in)

SIZES
0–6 months, sole length 9cm (3½in)
6–12 months, sole length 10cm (4in)

Note: Instructions are given for the smallest size first; the larger size is given in square brackets [ ]

STITCHES AND SKILLS
See Crochet Basics (pages 134–142)

Sole 1
Working in rounds
Working into front and back loops
Invdec
Crab stitch

To Make the Booties

(make 2)

Sole

Using MC make Sole 1.
Do not fasten off, but cont with the upper.

Upper

When working the CC1 yarn return the yarn back to the start of each round for that colour and then work over this strand with the contrast colour.

Round 1: 1 ch, miss st at base of 1 ch, 1 dc blo into each of next 45[49] sts, sl st into first dc to join.

Round 2: Working under both loops, 1 ch, 1 dc into each of next 11[13] sts, change to CC1, 1 dc into each of next 7 sts, change to MC, 1 dc into each of next 27[29] sts, sl st into first dc to join.

Round 3: 1 ch, 1 dc into each of next 12[14] sts, change to CC1, 1 dc into each of next 5 sts, change to MC, 1 dc into each of next 28[30] sts, sl st into first dc to join.

Round 4: 1 ch, 1 dc into each of next 13[15] sts, change to CC1, 1 dc into each of next 3 sts, change to MC, 1 dc into each of next 29[31] sts, sl st into first dc to join.

Round 5: 1 ch, 1 dc into each of next 3[5] sts, *Invdec, 1 dc into next st; rep from * 7 more times, 1 dc into each of next 18[20] sts, sl st into first dc to join. (37[41] sts)

Round 6: 1 ch, 1 dc into each of next 3[5] sts, *Invdec 8 times, 1 dc into each of next 18[20] sts, sl st into first dc to join. (29[33] sts) Fasten off. Weave ends into WS.

Face

Using CC1.

Foundation ring: 3 ch, sl st into 3rd ch from hook to join.

Round 1: 1 ch, 8 dc into the ring. (8 sts)

Cont to work in a spiral.

Round 2: 2 dc into each st. (16 sts)

HELPFUL TIP

Why not make a teddy bear version of this pattern using beige yarn? A super cute addition to any baby wardrobe.

Round 3: *1 dc into next st, 2 dc into next st; rep from * 7 more times. (24 sts)

Round 4: *1 dc into each of next 2 sts, 2 dc into next st; rep from * 7 more times. (32 sts)

Round 5: 1 ch, work 1 crab st into each st. Fasten off.

Ears

(make 2 per bootie)

Using MC.
Foundation ring: Make 3 ch, sl st into 3rd ch from hook to join.

Round 1: 3 ch, 5 dtr into the ring.

Fasten off leaving a tail.

HELPFUL TIP

Use the photograph on this page as a guide when finishing the facial details for the panda booties.

Eyes

(make 2 per bootie)

Using MC.
Foundation ring: 3 ch, sl st into 3rd ch from hook to join.

Round 1: 1 ch, 8 dc into the ring, sl st into first dc to join. (8 sts)

Fasten off leaving a tail.

Finishing

Sew around the edge of the white tummy using chain st and a strand of CC1. Using the photograph as a guide, sew the ears on to the back of the face using the tail of yarn, then sew the eyes on to the face. Sew a small st in the centre of the eye for a pupil, using blue embroidery thread. Sew a nose and a mouth on the face using black embroidery thread or yarn. Sew the face on to the bootie, matching the lower edge to the edge of opening (most of the face will not be attached and will stand upright when booties are worn). Weave all ends into WS.

10
ROARING
LIONS

You don't need to go deep into the jungle to find these adorable lions – they like to live on little feet and keep them warm and cosy. Let your baby walk on the wild side with these bright booties. Grrrrrrr!!!

BEFORE YOU BEGIN

SKILL LEVEL
1

YOU WILL NEED
Debbie Bliss Mia DK 50g (1.75oz); 100m (109yds); 50% cotton/ 50% wool
1 in Buttermilk (19) = MC
1 in Corn (14) = CC1
1 in Peach (12) = CC2
Small amount of DK weight yarn in black = CC3
Small amount of DK weight yarn in white = CC4

Hook
4mm (US G/6)
Adjust hook size if necessary to achieve correct tension

Notions
Stitch marker
Yarn needle

TENSION
20 sts and 22 rows in dc to measure 10cm (4in)

SIZES
0–6 months, sole length 9cm (3½in)
6–12 months, sole length 10cm (4in)

Note: Instructions are given for the smallest size first; the larger size is given in square brackets [ ]

STITCHES AND SKILLS
See Crochet Basics (pages 134–142)

Working in rows
Working in rounds
Working into front and back loops

To Make the Booties

(make 2)

Toe

Using MC, work in a spiral.

Round 1: Make 3[4] ch, 2 dc into 2nd ch from hook, 1 dc into next 0[1] ch, 4 dc into ch, working into opposite side of ch, 1 dc into next 0[1] ch, 2 dc into ch that already contains 2 dc. (8[10] sts)

Round 2: 2 dc into first st, 1 dc into each of next 2[3] sts, 2 dc into each of next 2 sts, 1 dc into each of next 2[3] sts, 2 dc into last st. (12[14] sts)

Round 3: 2 dc into first st, 1 dc into each of next 4[5] sts, 2 dc into each next 2 sts, 1 dc into each of next 4[5] sts, 2 dc into last st. (16[18] sts)

Round 4: 2 dc into each of first 2 sts, 1 dc into each of next 6[7] sts, 2 dc into each of next 2 sts, 1 dc into each of next 6[7] sts. (20[22] sts)

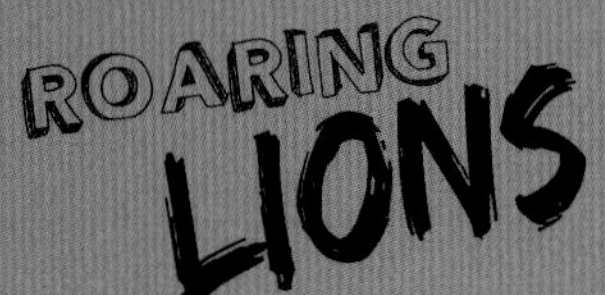

Rounds 5–7: 1 dc into each st. (20[22] sts)

Round 8: 1 dc into first 11 sts, 1 dc blo into each of next 9[11] sts. (20[22] sts)

Round 9: 1 dc blo into each of first 4 sts, 1 dc into each of next 7 sts, 1 dc blo into each of next 9[11] sts. (20[22] sts)

Round 10: 1 dc blo into each of first 4 sts, 1 dc into each of next 16[18] sts. (20[22] sts)

For larger size only: Round 11: 1 dc into each st. ([22] sts)

Body

Cont in MC.
Work in rows.

Row 1: 1 dc into each of next 16[17] sts, turn leaving rem 4[5] sts unworked, turn. (16[17] sts)

Row 2: 1 ch, 1 dc into each of next 15[16] sts, leaving rem st unworked, turn. (15[16] sts)

Row 3: 1 ch, 1 dc into each st, turn. (15[16] sts)

Rows 4–11: Rep Row 3. (15[16] sts)

For larger size only: Rep Row 3 twice more. ([16] sts)

Back Seam

Fold the back seam in half with RS together. Working through flo of the piece closest to you and blo of the piece farthest away from you, attach the two sides together by making a sl st though both layers into each of the next 7[8] sts. Fasten off.

Edging Rows

Using MC.
Round 1: With RS facing, 1 dc evenly around the foot opening for a total of 26[31] sts. Sl st into first dc to join. (26 [31] sts)

For larger size only: 1 dc into each st. ([31] sts)

Fasten off and weave ends into WS.

Mane

The blo sts in Rounds 8–10 of the bootie will form 2 lines of front loops over the top of the bootie. You will be working into these front loops to create the mane.

To make the first round of the mane, join CC1 by making a sl st into the bottom right front loop (bottom left if you are left-handed), *4 dc into the next st, sl st into the next st; rep from * 5[6] more times. Fasten off and weave ends into WS.

To make the second round of the mane, join the CC2 by making a sl st into the top right front loop (top left if you are left-handed), *4 htr into next st, sl st into next st; rep from * 5[6] more times. Fasten off and weave ends into WS.

Finishing

Nose

Using CC4, sew over the initial chain and into the sts of Round 1 of the bootie to create 2 white triangles. With CC3 yarn, create an upside-down triangle between the two white triangles, using the photograph as a guide.

Eyes

Fold the bootie flat so that the top is facing you. Mark the position of the eyes on Round 5 of the bootie, and in line with the outside edges of the nose. Add the eyes by making a couple of back sts for each eye, using CC3.

Tail

Using MC.
Make 8 ch, working into the back bump of the chain sts, sl st into 2nd ch from the hook and sl st into rem ch. Fasten off, leaving a 15cm (6in) tail. Sew the tail to the middle of the back seam using the tail of yarn, and weave ends into WS.

Tassel

Cut 3 or 4 pieces of CC2 approx 15cm (6in) long. Jab the hook through the end of the tail. Fold the pieces of yarn in half and grab them with the hook. Pull up a loop with all the pieces of yarn. Yarn over again (with all the pieces of yarn), and pull them all the way through the loop. Trim the tassel.

11
BABY
ELEPHANTS

Take a trip to the zoo in these whimsical elephant booties. Totally charming with little legs and large elephant ears, these booties are simple to make as the trunk and body are worked in one piece.

BEFORE YOU BEGIN

SKILL LEVEL
2

YOU WILL NEED
Debbie Bliss Rialto DK 50g (1.75oz); 105m (115yds); 100% merino wool
1 in Duck Egg (19) = MC
1 in Aqua (44) = CC1
Small amount of black yarn = CC2
Small amount of Citrus (69) = CC3

Hook
2.5mm (see note, page 135)
Adjust hook size if necessary to achieve correct tension

Notions
Polyester fibre filling (small amount for stuffing)
Stitch marker
Yarn needle

TENSION
11 sts and 8 rows in htr to measure 5cm (2in)

SIZES
0–6 months, sole length 9cm (3½in)
6–12 months, sole length 10cm (4in)

Note: Instructions are given for the smallest size first; the larger size is given in square brackets [ ]

STITCHES AND SKILLS
See Crochet Basics (pages 134–142)

Working in rows
Working in rounds
Working into front and back loops
Magic loop
dc2tog
Invdec

NOTE
Booties are crocheted in rounds that are not joined.
1 ch at beg of row does not count as a st. After 1 ch, work first dc into the same st.

To Make the Booties

(make 2)

Trunk

Using MC.
Round 1: 6 dc into a magic loop, pull magic loop to close shut.(6 sts)

Cont to work in a spiral.

Round 2: 2 dc into first st, 1 dc into each of next 5 sts. (7 sts)

Round 3: 2 dc into first st, 1 dc into each of next 6 sts. (8 sts)

Rounds 4–5: 1 dc into each st.

Round 6: 2 dc into first st, 1 dc into each of next 7 sts. (9 sts)

Round 7: 2 dc into first st, 1 dc into each of next 8 sts. (10 sts)

Round 8: 2 dc into first st, 1 dc into each of next 9 sts. (11 sts)

Round 9: 2 dc into first st, 1 dc into each of next 10 sts. (12 sts)

Rounds 10–11: 1 dc into each st.

Round 12: 2 dc into first st, 1 dc into each of next 11 sts. (13 sts)

Rounds 13–15: 1 dc into each st.

Round 16: 2 dc into each of next 7 sts, 1 dc into each of next 6 sts. (20 sts)

Round 17: 1 dc into each st.

Round 18: 2 dc into each of next 3 sts, 1 dc into each of next 4 sts, 2 dc into each of next 6 sts, 1 dc into each of next 4 sts, 2 dc into each of next 3 sts. (32 sts)

Rounds 19–20: 1 dc into each st.

Round 21: 1 dc into each of next 4 sts, 2 dc into next st, 1 dc into each of next 7 sts, 2 dc into next st, 1 dc into each of next 19 sts. (34 sts)

Rounds 22–27: 1 dc into each st.

Round 28: 1 dc into each of next 4 sts, Invdec over next 2 sts, 1 dc into each of next 7 sts, Invdec over next 2 sts, 1 dc into each of next 19 sts. (32 sts)

For larger size only: work 2 rows more of 1 dc into each st.

Round 29[31]: 1 dc into each st. (32 sts)

Round 30[32]: 1 dc into each of next 26 sts then switch to CC1, 1 dc into each of next 6 sts (so colour change will be on the sole) 1 dc into each of next 7 sts, turn.

Now work in rows.

Rows 1–9: 1 ch, 1 dc into each of next 24 sts, turn.

Row 10: 1 ch, 1 dc into each of next 9 sts, dc2tog 3 times, 1 dc into each of next 9 sts, turn. (21 sts)

Row 11: 1 ch, 1 dc into each of next 6 sts, dc2tog, 1 dc into each of next 5 sts, dc2tog, 1 dc into each of next 6 sts, turn. (19 sts)

Row 12: 1 ch, 1 dc into each of next 6 sts, dc2tog, 1 dc into each of next 3 sts, dc2tog, 1 dc into each of next 6 sts.

Cont with edging as follows: work around all 3 sides of the bootie with dc, working 1 dc into each row end and each st.

Join back seam as follows: fold WS together and join first 4 sts of sides with dc under both loops of each set of sts. Then cont with sl st, under two middle loops only, into last sts.

Ears

(make 2 per bootie)

Using MC.
Leave a tail of yarn for sewing up before making the magic loop.

Round 1: 6 dc into a magic loop, pull magic loop to close shut. (6 sts)

Cont to work in a spiral.

Round 2: 2 dc into each st. (12 sts)

Round 3: *2 dc into first st, 1 dc into next st; rep from * to end. (18 sts)

Switch to CC1.

Round 4: 1 dc into each st. (18 sts)

Fold the ear together, join the top edge together by working dc under 2 middle loops, to create little 'ridges' on the front of the ear, along the next 8 sts. For best results, make one more dc at the end of the row to create nice neat ears for both sides. Fasten off and weave ends into WS.

Eyes

(make 2 per bootie)

Using CC2.
Round 1: 6 dc into a magic loop, pull magic loop to close shut. (6 sts)

Switch to CC3 and cont to work in a spiral.

Round 2: 2 dc into each of next 5 sts, 1 dc into next st, sl st into first dc to join. Fasten off leaving a tail end.

Legs

(make 4 per bootie)

Using CC3.
Round 1: 6 dc into a magic loop, pull magic loop to close shut. (6 sts)

Cont to work in a spiral.

Round 2: *2 dc into next st, 1 dc into next st; rep from * to end. (9 sts)

Switch to CC1.

Round 3: 1 dc blo into each st.

Round 4: 1 dc into each st.

Round 5: 1 dc into each of next 8 sts, sl st into last st. Fasten off, leaving a long tail to attach the leg to the body. Stuff lightly.

Finishing

Start joining the legs to the bottom of the sole, placing legs as follows: sit the bootie on a flat, level surface in order to place the legs evenly. Fold the bootie flat and mark the position for the legs with a pin, using the photograph as a guide. Start sewing and, if needed, flatten the bootie again to see where to place the next leg. Using this method will ensure that the legs are all on the same line and evenly placed. Weave ends into WS and trim. Using tail end of yarn, attach eyes to the bootie, refer to the photograph as a guide. Using yarn in MC, attach ears to bootie, refer to the photograph as a guide.

HELPFUL TIPS

Hand-wash in cold water, pat dry, do not wring. Air-dry.

12
SNAPPY
CROCS

See you later, alligator! Your little one will be the snappiest dresser in town with these jaunty reptile booties. A simple project to crochet up for booties with a real bite.

BEFORE YOU BEGIN

SKILL LEVEL
2

YOU WILL NEED
Debbie Bliss Rialto DK 50g (1.75oz); 105m (115yds); 100% merino wool
1 in Apple = MC
1 in Citrus = CC1
Small amount of pale green yarn = CC2

Hook
2.5mm (see note, page 135)
Adjust hook size if necessary to achieve correct tension

Notions
Stitch marker
Yarn needle

TENSION
11 sts and 8 rows in htr to measure 5cm (2in)

SIZES
0–6 months, sole length 9cm (3½in)
6–12 months, sole length 10cm (4in)

Note: Instructions are given for the smallest size first; the larger size is given in square brackets [ ]

STITCHES AND SKILLS
See Crochet Basics (pages 134–142)

Working in rows
Working in rounds
Working into front and back loops
Magic loop
Invdec

NOTE
1 ch at beg of row does not count as a st. After 1 ch, work first dc into the same st.

To Make the Booties

(make 2)

Body

Using MC.
Round 1: 6 dc into a magic loop, pull magic loop to close shut. (6 sts)

Cont to work in a spiral.

Round 2: 2 dc into each st. (12 sts)

Round 3: 1 dc into each st.

Round 4: *2 dc into next st, 1 dc into each of next 5 sts; rep from * once more. (14 sts)

Round 5: 1 dc into each st.

Round 6: *2 dc into next st, 1 dc into each of next 6 sts; rep from * once more. (16 sts)

Round 7: *2 dc into next st, 1 dc into each of next 7 sts; rep from * once more. (18 sts)

Round 8: *2 dc into each of next 2 sts, 1 dc into each of next 7 sts; rep from * once more. (22 sts)

Round 9: *2 dc into each of next 3 sts, 1 dc into each of next 2 sts, 2 dc into each of next 4 sts, 1 dc into each of next 2 sts, 2 dc into each of next 3 sts, 1 dc into each of next 8 sts. (32 sts)

Rounds 10–12: 1 dc into each st.

Round 13: 1 dc into each of next 4 sts, 2 dc into next st, 1 dc into each of next 12 sts, 2 dc into next st, 1 dc into each of next 14 sts. (34 sts)

Round 14: 1 dc into each st.

For larger size only: Rep Round 14 once more.

Round 15[16]: 1 dc into each of next 4 sts, Invdec over next 2 sts, 1 dc into each of next 14 sts, Invdec over next 2 sts, 1 dc into each of next 12 sts. (32 sts)

Round 16[17]: 1 dc into each st.

For larger size only: Rep Round 14 once more.

Round 17[19]: 1 dc into each of next 9 sts, turn, cont in rows.

Rows 1–9: 1 ch, 1 dc into each of next 24 sts, turn.

Row 10: 1 ch, 1 dc into each of next 24 sts, do not turn but continue working in rounds. Mark the new beginning of the round.

Round 11: 9 ch, 1 dc into each of next 24 sts.

Round 12: 1 dc into each of next 9 sts of ch, 1 dc into each of next 24 sts. (33 sts)

Round 13: *Invdec over next 2 sts, 1 dc into next st; rep from * 5 more times, 1 dc into each of next 15 sts. (27 sts)

Round 14: 1 dc into each of next 6 sts, Invdec over next 2 sts, 1 dc into each of next 19 sts. (26 sts)

Round 15: 1 dc into each of next 24 sts, Invdec over next 2 sts. (25 sts)

Round 16: *Invdec over next 2 sts, 1 dc into next st; rep from * twice more, 1 dc into each of next 14 sts, Invdec over next 2 sts. (21 sts)

Round 17: *Invdec over next 2 sts, 1 dc into next st; rep from * once more, 1 dc into each of next 13 sts, Invdec over next 2 sts. (18 sts)

Round 18: *Invdec over next 2 sts, 1 dc into next st; rep from * once more, 1 dc into each of next 12 sts. (15 sts)

Round 19: 1 dc into each of next 3 sts, Invdec over next 2 sts, 1 dc into each of next 10 sts. (14 sts)

Round 20: 1 dc into each of next 3 sts, Invdec over next 2 sts, 1 dc into each of next 9 sts. (13 sts)

Round 21: 1 dc into each of next 3 sts, Invdec over next 2 sts, 1 dc into each of next 8 sts. (12 sts)

Round 22: 1 dc into each of next 3 sts, Invdec over next 2 sts, 1 dc into each of next 7 sts. (11 sts)

Round 23: 1 dc into each of next 3 sts, Invdec over next 2 sts, 1 dc into each of next 6 sts. (10 sts)

Round 24: 1 dc into each of next 3 sts, Invdec over next 2 sts, 1 dc into each of next 5 sts. (9 sts)

Round 25: 1 dc into each of next 3 sts, *Invdec over next 2 sts; rep from * once more, 1 dc into each of next 2 sts. (7 sts)

Round 26: 1 dc into each of next 2 sts, *Invdec over next 2 sts; rep from * once more, sl st into last st. (5 sts)

For a neat finish, 5 sc are left at the end. Cut the yarn and thread on to a yarn needle, thread

through rem dc, one at a time and gather them together. Secure gathers with a knot and fasten off, weaving ends into WS.

Edging

Using MC, start crocheting around the upper part of the shoe as follows: starting from one side, make 1 dc into each of next 11 sts, then (along one side of the face) *Invdec over next 2 sts; rep from * 4 more times, 1 dc into each of next 11 sts on the other side, working across the back, 1 dc into each of next 3 sts, Invdec over next 2 sts, 1 dc into each of next 3 sts, sl st into first dc to join. Fasten off and weave ends into WS.

Eyes

(make 2 per bootie)

Using CC2.
Round 1: 6 dc into a magic loop, pull magic loop to close shut. (6 sts)

Switch to CC1 and cont to work in a spiral.

Round 2: 2 dc into each of next 6 sts. (12 sts)

Switch to MC and cont.

Round 3: 1 dc into each of next 11 sts, sl st into last st.

Fasten off leaving a long tail to attach the eye on to the bootie.

Legs

(make 4 per bootie – 2 legs using MC, 2 legs using CC1)
Round 1: 6 dc into a magic loop, pull magic loop to close shut. (6 sts)

Cont to work in a spiral.

Round 2: 2 dc into each of next 5 sts, 1 dc into last st. (11 sts)

Round 3: *Invdec over next 2 sts; rep from * once more, 1 dc into each of next 7 sts. (9 sts)

Round 4: *Invdec over next 2 sts; rep from * once more, 1 dc into each of next 4 sts, sl st into last st. (7 sts)

Fasten off, leaving a long tail to attach the leg to the body.

Finishing

Start joining each leg to the bottom of the sole, placing legs as follows: sit the bootie on a flat, level surface in order to place the legs evenly. Fold the bootie flat and mark the position for the legs with a pin, using the photograph as a guide. Start sewing and, if needed, flatten the bootie again to see where to place next leg. Using this method will ensure that the legs are all on the same line and evenly placed. Weave ends into WS and trim.

Finally, make the nostril and claw details as follows: for one detail, sew a small horizontal st. Keep sewing over that st until you have achieved the desired definition; the more times you stitch over, the larger the nostril or claw you will have.

13 HAMMERHEAD SHARKS

Your baby will make a splash with this friendly pair, especially when wriggling toes reveal the smiley face embroidered on the underside of the toe section. These realistic shark booties are made in sections and joined together.

BEFORE YOU BEGIN

SKILL LEVEL
3

YOU WILL NEED
Cascade 220 Sport 50g (1.75oz); 150m (164yds); 100% Peruvian highland wool
1 in Silver Grey (8401) = MC
1 in White (8505) = CC1
1 in Charcoal Gray (8400) = CC2

Hook
3.5mm (US E/4)
Adjust hook size if necessary to achieve correct tension

Notions
Stitch marker
Yarn needle

TENSION
9 sts and 11 rows in dc to measure 5cm (2in)

SIZES
0–6 months, sole length 9cm (3½in)
6–12 months, sole length 10cm (4in)

Note: Instructions are given for the smallest size first; the larger size is given in square brackets [ ]

STITCHES AND SKILLS
See Crochet Basics (pages 134–142)

Working in rows
Working in rounds
dc2tog

NOTE
Head, tail and fins are the same for both sizes.

To Make the Booties

(make 2)

Head

Using MC.
Row 1: Make 16 ch, 1 dc into 2nd ch from hook, 1 dc into each rem ch, turn. (15 sts)

Rows 2–5: 1 ch, 1 dc into each st, turn. (15 sts)

Switch to CC1 during last dc of Row 5.

Row 6: 1 ch, 1 dc into flo of each st, turn. (15 sts)

Row 7–12: 1 ch, 1 dc into each st, turn. (15 sts)

Fasten off. Weave ends into WS.

Fold the head in half, sew each end together and sew 4 sts in from each end, leaving the middle 7 sts unsewn.

Next, using the photograph as a guide, sew a mouth on to the centre of CC1 with MC yarn. Sew eyes to either side of the head with CC2 yarn.

HAMMERHEAD SHARKS

Body
Using MC.
Round 1: Join MC to top centre of MC from head. 1 ch, 1 dc into each unsewn st around head, sl st into first dc to join. (14 sts)

Round 2: 1 ch, 1 dc into each st. (14 sts)

Cont to work in a spiral.

Round 3: 2 dc into next st, 1 dc into each of next 12 sts, 2 dc into last st. (16 sts)

Round 4: 2 dc into next st, 1 dc into each of next 14 sts, 2 dc into last st. (18 sts)

Round 5: 2 dc into next st, 1 dc into each of next 16 sts, 2 dc into last st. (20 sts)

Rounds 6–7: 1 dc into each st, turn.

Now work in rows.

Rows 8–19[23]: 1 ch, 1 dc into each of next 20 sts, turn. (20 sts)

Row 20[24]: 1 ch, 1 dc into each of next 7 sts, dc2tog 3 times, 1 dc into each of next 7 sts. (17 sts)

Fasten off, leaving a long tail. Fold the top edge (last row) in half and using a yarn needle, sew the edges together.

Tail
(make 2 per bootie)

Using MC.
Row 1: Make 6 ch, 1 dc into 2nd ch from hook, 1 dc into each rem ch turn. (5 sts)

Row 2: 1 ch, 2 dc into next st, 1 dc into each of next 3 sts, 2 dc into last st, turn. (7 sts)

Row 3: 1 ch, 2 dc into next st, 1 dc into each of next 5 sts, 2 dc into last st, turn. (9 sts)

Row 4: 1 ch, 2 dc into next st, 1 dc into each of next 7 sts, 2 dc into last st, turn. (11 sts)

Cont with Right Side of Tail.

Right Side of Tail
Row 5: 1 ch, 1 dc into each of next 4 sts, dc2tog, turn, leaving rem sts unworked. (5 sts)

Row 6: 1 ch, 1 dc into each st, turn. (5 sts)

Row 7: 1 ch, 1 dc into each of next 3 sts, dc2tog, turn. (4 sts)

Row 8: 1 ch, 1 dc into each st, turn. (4 sts)

Row 9: 1 ch, dc2tog twice, turn. (2 sts)

Row 10: 1 ch, 1 dc into each st, turn. (2 sts)

Row 11: 1 ch, dc2tog. (1 st)

Fasten off. Weave ends into WS.

Left Side of Tail

Row 5: Join yarn into next unworked st on Row 5 of Right Side of Tail, 1 dc into same st, dc2tog, 1 dc into each of next 2 sts, turn. (4 sts)

Row 6: 1 ch, 1 dc into each st, turn. (4 sts)

Row 7: 1 ch, dc2tog, 1 tr into each of next 2 sts. (3 sts)

Fasten off. Weave ends into WS.

Using a yarn needle, sew the two tails together, leaving the first row of each side unsewn. Now work in rounds.

Round 1: Join yarn into any st, 1 dc around first rows of tail, do not join. (10 sts)

Round 2: 2 dc into each st, sl st into first dc to join. Fasten off, leaving a long tail. (20 sts)

Using a yarn needle, sew the tail over the seam on the body, working over each st to make it appear seamless.

Top Fin

Using MC.

Round 1: 2 ch, 3 dc into 2nd ch from hook, do not join. (3 sts)

Cont to work in a spiral.

Round 2: 2 dc into each st. (6 sts)

Round 3: *1 dc into next st, 2 dc into next st; rep from * twice more. (9 sts)

Rounds 4–5: 1 dc into each st. (9 sts)

Round 6: 1 dc into each of next 4 sts, 1 tr into each of next 5 sts. (9 sts)

Round 7: 1 dc into each of next 4 sts, 1 tr into each of next 5 sts, sl st into first dc to join. (9 sts)

Fasten off, leaving a long tail. Using a yarn needle, sew the fin into front centre of the foot hole.

Side Fins

(make 1 in each of MC and CC1 per bootie)

Row 1: 5 ch, 1 dc into 2nd ch from hook, 1 dc into each rem ch, turn. (4 sts)

Rows 2–4: 1 ch, 1 dc into each st. (4 sts)

Row 5: 1 ch, dc2tog twice, turn. (2 sts)

Row 6: 1 ch, 1 dc into each st, turn. (2 sts)

Row 7: 1 ch, dc2tog. (1 st)

Fasten off, weave ends into WS. Using MC, sew MC and CC1 side fins together. Keep an eye on the shape of your fins, sewing each set so that each side of the shark matches. Using MC, sew fins on to shark.

Foot Trim

All sizes.

Join MC with a sl st at back seam, 1 ch, using ends of rows as sts 1 dc into each st, sl st into first dc to join. Fasten off and weave ends into WS.

14
OCTO
TOES

Brighten up your baby's day with these zingy cuffed boots. Pick up your hook and dive straight in! For a different twist, try making the booties in pink for a squishy squid variation.

BEFORE YOU BEGIN

SKILL LEVEL
1

YOU WILL NEED
Cascade 220 Sport 50g (1.75oz); 150m (164yds); 100% Peruvian highland wool
1 in Blue Hawaii (9421) = MC
Small amount of Orange Sherbert (7825) = CC1
Small amount of black yarn = CC2

Hook
3.75mm (US F/5)
Adjust hook size if necessary to achieve correct tension

Notions
Black embroidery thread
Stitch marker
Yarn needle

TENSION
11 sts and 8 rows in htr to measure 5cm (2in)

SIZES
0–6 months, sole length 9cm (3½in)
6–12 months, sole length 10cm (4in)

Note: Instructions are given for the smallest size first; the larger size is given in square brackets [ ]

STITCHES AND SKILLS
See Crochet Basics (pages 134–142)

Sole 1
Working in rounds
Working into back loops
dc2tog

NOTES
When working in rounds, work first st(s) into same st as sl st join. First 1 ch does not count as a st.

To Make the Booties

(make 2)

Sole

Using MC, make Sole 1.

Fasten off then re-attach yarn to centre back st. Cont with upper.

Upper

Round 1: 1 ch, 1 htr into blo of each st, sl st into first htr to join. (46[50] sts)

Round 2: 1 ch, 1 dc into each of first 11[12] sts, 1 htr into each of next 24[26] sts, 1 dc into each of next 11[12] sts, sl st into first dc to join. (46[50] sts)

Round 3: Rep Round 2.

Round 4: 1 ch, 1 dc into each st, sl st into first dc to join.

Round 5: 1 ch, 1 dc into each of first 14[15] sts, *dc2tog, 1 dc into each of next 2 sts; rep from * 3[4] more times, dc2tog 1[0] times, 1 dc into each of next 14[15] sts, sl st into first st to join. (41[45] sts)

Round 6: 1 ch, 1 dc into each of first 16[17] sts, *dc2tog, 1 dc into next st; rep from * twice more, dc2tog 0[1] times, 1 dc into each of next 16[17] sts, sl st into first st to join. (38[41] sts)

Round 7: 1 ch, 1 dc into each of first 12[13] sts, dc2tog 7[8] times, 1 dc into each of next 12 sts, sl st into first st to join. (31[33] sts)

Round 8: 1 ch, 1 dc into each of first 12[13] sts, dc2tog 4 times, 1 dc into each of next 11[12] sts, sl st into first st to join. (27[29] sts)

Round 9: 1 ch, 1 dc into each of first 12[13] sts, dc2tog twice, 1 dc into each of next 11[12] sts, sl st into first st to join. (25[27] sts)

Round 10: 1 ch, 1 dc into each st, sl st into first st to join.

Rounds 11–12: Rep Round 10.

Switch to CC1.

Round 13: 1 ch, 1 htr into each st, sl st into first htr to join. (25[27] sts)

Rounds 14–22: Rep Round 13 9 more times.

Round 23: *(10 ch, 2 dc into 2nd ch from hook, 2 dc into each of next 8 ch, sl st into same st of Round 22 at base of 10 ch*, 1 dc into each of next 2 sts, sl st into next st; rep between * and * once more, 1 dc into each of next 2[3] sts, sl st into next st); rep between (and) twice more; rep between * and * once more, 1 dc into each of next 2 sts, sl st into next st, rep between * and * once more, 1 dc into each of next 2 sts, sl st into first ch. (8 legs)

Fasten off, weave ends into WS.

Finishing

Turn the top of the bootie over to RS. Using black yarn, embroider the face through both layers of fabric.

15
WONDERFUL
WHALES

Let these teeny tiny whale booties protect your little one's feet when they are off on their high-sea adventures. The laces double as the whale's spout – embroider a wide smile for added cuteness.

BEFORE YOU BEGIN

SKILL LEVEL
2

YOU WILL NEED
Sirdar Snuggly DK 50g (1.75oz); 165m (179yds); 55% nylon/ 45% acrylic
1 in Peaceful (188) = MC
Small amount of white yarn = CC1

Hook
3.25mm (US D/3)
Adjust hook size if necessary to achieve correct tension

Notions
Black embroidery thread
Stitch marker
Yarn needle

TENSION
10 sts and 12 rows in dc to measure 5cm (2in)

SIZES
0–6 months, sole length 9cm (3½in)
6–12 months, sole length 10cm (4in)

Note: Instructions are given for the smallest size first; the larger size is given in square brackets [ ]

STITCHES AND SKILLS
See Crochet Basics (pages 134–142)

Working in rounds
Magic loop
dc2tog
htr2tog

NOTES
Sl st into first st to join rounds.
First 1 ch does not count as a st.
When working in rounds, make first st(s) into same st as sl st join.

To Make the Booties

(make 2)

Sole

Using MC.

Round 1: Make 11[13] ch, 1 htr into 3rd ch from hook, 1 htr into each of next 7[9] sts, 6 htr into last ch, working on opposite side, 1 htr into each of next 7[9] sts, 5 htr into last ch, sl st into first htr to join. (26[30] sts)

HELPFUL TIP

To make sure that it can't be pulled off by little hands, secure one side of the spout (laces) to the bootie with a couple of tack stitches.

Round 2: 1 ch, 1 htr into each of next 8[10] sts, 2 htr into each of next 5 sts, 1 htr into next 8[10] sts, 2 htr into each of next 5 sts, sl st into first htr to join. (36[40] sts)

Round 3: 1 ch, 1 htr into each of next 8[10] sts, *2 htr into next st, 1 htr into next st; rep from * 4 more times, 1 htr into each of next 8[10] sts, rep from * 5 more times, sl st into first htr to join. Cont with upper. (46[50] sts)

Upper

For each round make first dc into same st as sl st.

Rounds 1–4: 1 ch, 1 dc into each st, sl st into first dc to join. (46[50] sts)

Round 5: 1 ch, 1 dc into each of next 8[10] sts, *htr2tog, 1 htr into next st, rep from * 5 more times, 1 dc into each of next 20[22] sts, sl st into first dc to join. (40[44] sts)

Round 6: 1 ch, 1 dc into each of next 8[10] sts, *htr2tog, 1 htr into next st, rep from * 3 more times, 1 dc into each of next 20[22] sts, sl st into first dc to join. (36[40] sts)

Round 7: 1 ch, 1 dc into each of next 4[6] sts, 2 ch, miss next st, 1 dc into each of next 14[13] sts, 2 ch, miss next st, 1 dc into each of next 16[19] sts, sl st into first dc to join.

Fasten off and weave ends into WS.

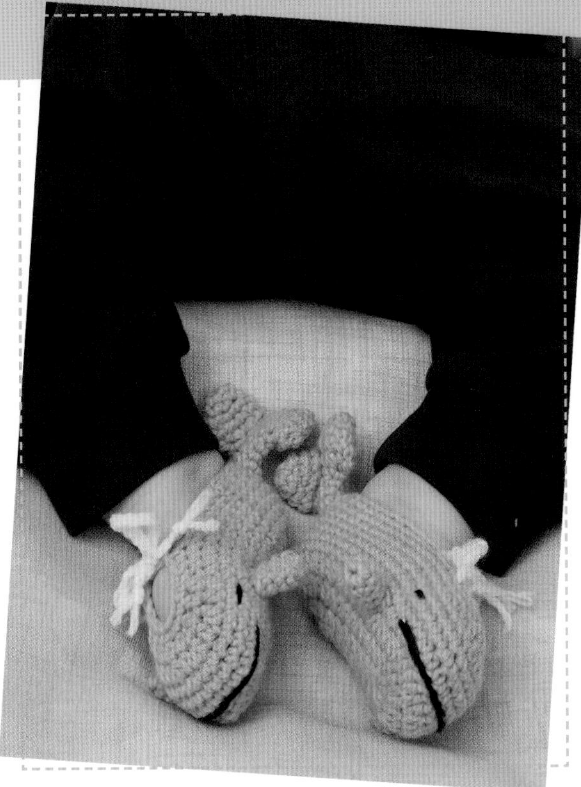

Spouts (Laces)

Using CC1.

Cut 3 pieces, 25cm (10in) each. Holding the 3 strands together tie a knot on one end leaving about 1.25cm (½in) of ends. Braid the strands and tie a knot leaving about 1.25cm (½in) of ends, trim for neater finish if desired. Thread through 2 ch space from Round 7 of shoe upper and tie together.

Note: Tail flukes are worked separately in rounds, then joined.

Tail

Using MC.

Round 1: 6 dc into a magic loop, pull magic loop to close shut, sl st into first dc to join. (6 sts)

Round 2: 1 ch, 1 dc into each st, sl st into first dc to join. (6 sts)

Round 3: 1 ch, 2 dc into each st, sl st into first dc to join. (12 sts)

Round 4: 1 ch, 1 dc into each st, sl st into first dc to join. (12 sts)

Fasten off and weave ends into WS.

Make the second fluke following Rounds 1–4 but do not fasten off, complete as follows working in continuous spirals. Use a stitch marker to keep track of rounds.

Round 1: Insert hook into what would be next st of first fluke and dc2tog 6 times, do not cut yarn. Continuing on to 2nd fluke, dc2tog 6 times. (12 sts)

Round 2: Dc2tog, 1 dc into each of next 3 sts, dc2tog, 1 dc into each of next 5 sts. (10 sts)

Rounds 3–5: 1 dc into each st.

Fasten off and leave long tail for sewing to the back of shoe upper.

Fins

(make 2 per bootie)

Round 1: 6 dc into a magic loop, pull magic loop to close shut, sl st into first dc to join. (6 sts)

Round 2: 1 ch, 1 dc into each st, join with sl st into first dc.

Rep Round 2 twice more. Fasten off and leave tail for sewing to the side of the bootie.

Finishing

Sew tail to the back of the bootie. Sew fins on to each side of the toe. Embroider eyes and a mouth with black embroidery thread, using the photograph as a guide.

CUTE CREATURES

16
BAA BAA
BOOTIES

With their sheepish expression and curly wool coat, these charming sheep shoes are full of fun. The toe is worked in the round and rows are used to create the sole and the sides.

BEFORE YOU BEGIN

SKILL LEVEL
2

YOU WILL NEED
Debbie Bliss Baby Cashmerino
50g (1.75oz); 125m (136yds);
33% microfibre/55% wool/
12% cashmere
1 in Ecru (101) = MC
Small amount of Clotted Cream
(65) = CC1

Hook
3.5mm (US E/4)
Adjust hook size if necessary to achieve correct tension

Notions
Black embroidery thread
Stitch marker
Yarn needle

TENSION
10 sts and 10 rows in dc to measure 5cm (2in)

SIZES
0–6 months, sole length 9cm (3½in)
6–12 months, sole length 10cm (4in)

Note: Instructions are given for the smallest size first; the larger size is given in square brackets [ ]

STITCHES AND SKILLS
See Crochet Basics (pages 134–142)

Working in rows
Working in rounds
Working into front and back loops
dc2tog

To Make the Booties

(make 2)

Toe

Using MC.

Foundation ring: Make 4 ch, sl st into first ch to join.

Round 1: 1 ch, 8 dc into the ring, sl st into first dc to join. (8 sts)

Cont to work in a spiral.

Round 2: 2 dc into each st. (16 sts)

Little hands will love the woollen hair and cute ears, so make sure all components are securely fastened to the main bootie.

Round 3: *1 dc into next st, 2 dc into next st; rep from * to end. (24 sts)

Rounds 4–5: 1 dc into each st. (24 sts)

Round 6: *1 dc into each of next 2 sts, 2 dc into next st; rep from * to end. (32 sts)

Rounds 7–9: 1 dc into each st. (32 sts)

Round 10: 1 dc into blo of each of next 8 sts, 1 sc into both loops of rem 24sts, turn. Do not fasten off.

You will now work in rows for the sides and the sole.

Sides and Sole

Row 1: 1 ch, 1 dc into each of next 24 sts, turn. (24 sts)

Rows 2–12: Rep Row 1 11 times.

For larger size only: Rows 13–14: Rep Row 1 twice more.

Fasten off.

Heel

Using MC.
Join yarn into 8th st from the right-hand heel edge.

Row 1: 1 ch, 1 dc into st at the base of ch, 1 dc into each of next 7 sts, turn. (8 sts)

Rows 2–8: Rep Row 1 7 more times. Fasten off.

With WS facing (turn the bootie inside out) and right sides together, place the heel and side edges together. Working through both layers, join two seams together with sl st. Fasten off and weave ends into WS.

Foot Edging

Using MC.
Round 1: Join MC with a sl st at the corner of the left-hand toe edge and Row 1 of the shoe side, 1 ch, work 10[12] dc evenly along the side, dc2tog across the corner of the side and the heel, 4 dc evenly across the top of the heel, dc2tog across the corner of the side and the heel, and work 10[12] dc evenly along the right-hand side edge. Fasten off and weave ends into WS.

Ears

(make 4)

Using MC.
Row 1: 4 ch, 2 dc into 2nd ch from hook, 1 dc into next ch, 2 dc into last ch, turn. (5 sts)

Row 2: 1 ch, 1 dc into each st, turn. (5 sts)

Row 3: 1 ch, dc2tog, 1 dc into each of next 3 sts, turn. (4 sts)

Row 4: 1 ch, 1 dc into each of next 2 sts, dc2tog. (3 sts)

Row 5: 1 ch, dc2tog, 1 dc into next st, turn. (2 sts)

Row 6: 1 ch, dc2tog. Fasten off, leaving a long tail of yarn.

Hair

You will work the hair as loops into the last two rows of the toe edge, across 8 dc at beg of opening. Work first row with toe of shoe facing.

Using CC1.

Row 1: Join CC1 with a sl st into flo of Round 9 of toe, *6 ch, sl st into flo of next st; rep from * 7 more times, turn.

Row 2: Working into Round 10 of toe only,*6 ch, sl st into blo of next st; rep from * 7 more times. Fasten off and weave ends into WS.

Finishing

Sew the ears either side of the hair using the tail of yarn and a yarn needle. Sew the eyes and nose using backstitch and black embroidery thread. Fasten off and weave ends into WS.

HELPFUL TIP

These booties would make an ideal baby shower gift. Make this gift extra special by covering a small box in wrapping paper. Stuff each bootie with white tissue paper, then finish the presentation box with a ribbon.

17

ADORABLE DUCKLINGS

These smart little shoes are full of vintage nursery charm. The cute faces form the instep of the shoe, and the embroidered eyes and crocheted beak add character. Quack! Quack!

BEFORE YOU BEGIN

SKILL LEVEL
1

YOU WILL NEED
Debbie Bliss Baby Cashmerino
50g (1.75oz); 125m (136 yds);
33% microfibre/55% wool/
12% cashmere
1 in Butter (83) = MC
Small amount of DK weight yarn in orange = CC1

Hook
3.5mm (US E/4)
Adjust hook size if necessary to achieve correct tension

Notions
Black embroidery thread
Stitch marker
Yarn needle

TENSION
10 sts and 10 rows in dc to measure 5cm (2in)

SIZES
0–6 months, sole length 9cm (3½in)
6–12 months, sole length 10cm (4in)

Note: Instructions are given for the smallest size first; the larger size is given in square brackets [ ]

STITCHES AND SKILLS
See Crochet Basics (pages 134–142)

Sole 1
Working in rounds
Working into front and back loops
dc2tog
Crab stitch

To Make the Booties

(make 2)

Sole

Using MC, make Sole 1.

Do not fasten off, but cont with upper.

Upper

Round 1: 1 ch, skip st at base of ch, 1 dc blo into each of next 45[49] sts, sl st into first dc to join.

Rounds 2–4: Working under both loops of every st, rep Round 1.

HELPFUL TIP

Get creative and try different colours to make a whole flock of birdie booties – choose sky blue for a bluebird.

Round 5: 1 ch, 1 dc into each of next 3[5] sts, *dc2tog flo, 1 dc into next st; rep from * 7 more times, 1 dc into each of next 18[20] sts, sl st into first dc to join. (37[41] sts)

Round 6: 1 ch, 1 dc into each of next 3[5] sts, dc2tog flo 8 times, 1 dc into each of next 18[20] sts, sl st into first dc to join. Fasten off. Weave ends into WS. (29[33] sts)

Tail

Using MC, join yarn into 21st st of upper (at centre back), skip next st, 5 tr into next st, skip next st, sl st into next st. Fasten off. Weave ends into WS.

Face

Using MC.
Foundation ring: Make 3 ch, sl st into first ch to join.

Round 1: 1 ch, 8 dc into the ring, sl st into first dc to join. (8 sts)

Cont to work in a spiral.

Round 2: 2 dc into each st. (16 sts)

Round 3: *1 dc into next st, 2 dc into next st; rep from * 7 more times. (24 sts)

Round 4: *1 dc into each of next 2 sts, 2 dc into next st; rep from * 7 more times. (32 sts)

Round 5: 1 ch, work 1 crab st into each st. Fasten off.

Beak

Using CC1.
Foundation ring: Make 3 ch, sl st into first ch to join.

Round 1: 1 ch, 4 dc into the ring, sl st into first dc to join. (4 sts)

Cont to work in a spiral.

Round 2: 2 dc into each st. (8 sts)

Round 3: 1 dc into each st. (8 sts)

Fasten off leaving a tail.

Feet

(make 2 per bootie)

Using CC1.
Foundation ring: Make 3 ch, sl st into first ch to join.

Round 1: 1 ch, 8 dc into the ring, sl st into first dc to join. (8 sts)

Cont to work in a spiral.

Round 2: 2 sc into each of the next 4 sts. (8 sts).

Fasten off leaving a tail.

Finishing

Using the photograph as a guide, sew the feet onto the base of the sole at the front of the bootie using the tail of yarn. Attach the beak to the center of the face. Add two eyes onto the face using black embroidery thread. Attach the face securely to the front of the bootie. Weave ends into WS.

HELPFUL TIP

To make wings, cut out two orange felt shapes and sew one to each side of the bootie.

18

Bunny Hop Toes

Hippity hop! These sleepy baby bunnies have long ears and a chubby tail – perfect for keeping little feet cosy. Pair with pjs for the perfect sleepy time outfit.

BEFORE YOU BEGIN

SKILL LEVEL
1

YOU WILL NEED
Debbie Bliss Rialto DK 50g (1.75oz); 105m (115yds); 100% merino wool
1 in Pink (42) = MC
1 in Sea Green (81) = CC1
Small amount of Light Grey (04) = CC2
Small amount of Light Blue (19) = CC3
Small amount of Light Rose (65) = CC4

Hook
2.5mm for 0–6 months
3.0mm for 6–12 months
(see note, page 135)
Adjust hook size if necessary to achieve correct tension

Notions
Black embroidery thread
Polyester fibre filling (small amount for stuffing)
Stitch marker
Yarn needle

TENSION
11 sts and 8 rows in htr to measure 5cm (2in) with 2.5mm hook
11 sts and 8 rows in htr to measure 5.5cm (2¼in) with 3.0mm hook

SIZES
0–6 months, sole length 9cm (3½in)
6–12 months, sole length 10cm (4in)

Note: Instructions are given for the smallest size first; the larger size is given in square brackets [ ]

STITCHES AND SKILLS
See Crochet Basics (pages 134–142)

Working in rounds
Working into back loops
Magic loop
Invdec

NOTES
CC1 yarn used in photographs is Grass (58), discontinued.
The first 1 ch does not count as a st. After first 1 ch, work first dc into same st.

To Make the Booties

(make 2)

Sole

Using CC1.

Round 1: Make 13 ch, 1 htr into 3rd ch from hook, 1 htr into each of next 9 ch, 6 htr into last ch, working on opposite side, 1 htr into each of next 9 ch, 5 htr into last ch, sl st into first htr to join. (30 sts)

Thoroughly weave in any ends to ensure a smart finish for the booties.

Round 2: 1 ch, 1 htr into each of next 10 sts, 2 htr in each of next 5 sts, 1 htr into each of next 10 sts, 2 htr into each of next 5 sts, sl st into first htr to join. (40 sts)

Round 3: 1 ch, 1 htr into each of next 10 sts, *2 htr into next st, 1 htr into next st*; rep from * to * 4 more times, 1 htr into each of next 10 sts; rep from * to * 5 more times, sl st into first htr to join. (50 sts)

Upper

Switch to MC and cont in rounds for upper.
Round 1: 1 ch, 1 dc blo into each of next 50 sts, sl st into first dc to join.

Rounds 2–5: 1 ch, 1 dc into each st, sl st into first dc to join.

Round 6: 1 ch, 1 dc into next st, *Invdec over next 2 sts, 1 dc into next st; rep from * 9 more times, 1 dc into each of next 9 sts, Invdec over next 2 sts, 1 dc into each of next 7 sts, sl st into first dc to join. (38 sts)

Round 7: 1 dc into each st, sl st into first dc to join. (38 sts)

Round 8: 1 dc into each of next 7 sts, *Invdec over next 2 sts; rep from * 3 more times, 1 dc into each of next 13 sts, Invdec over next 2 sts, 1 dc into next st, Invdec over next 2 sts, 1 dc into each of next 5 sts, sl st into first dc to join. (32 sts) Fasten off.

Ears

(make 2 per bootie)

Using CC1.
Round 1: 6 dc into a magic loop, pull magic loop to close shut. (6 sts)

Cont to work in a spiral.

Round 2: *2 dc into next st, 1 dc into next st; rep from * to end. (9 sts)

Round 3: *2 dc into next st, 1 dc into each of next 2 sts; rep from * to end. (12 sts)

Rounds 4–6: 1 dc into each st. (12 sts)

Round 7: *Invdec over next 2 sts; rep from * twice more, 1 dc into each of next 6 sts. (9 sts)

Round 8: *Invdec over next 2 sts; rep from * once more, 1 dc into each of next 4 sts, 1 sl st into last st. Fasten off leaving a long tail.

Eyes

(make 2 per bootie)

Using CC2.
Round 1: 6 dc into a magic loop, pull magic loop to close shut. (6 sts)

Cont to work in a spiral.

HELPFUL TIP

Make the bunnies wide-eyed and awake by embroidering a black circle in the middle of each eye.

Round 2: 2 dc into each of next 2 sts, 1 dc into each of next 2 sts, 2 dc into each of next 2 sts. (10 sts)

Round 3: 1 dc into each of next 2 sts, 2 dc into each of next 2 sts, 1 dc into each of next 2 sts, 2 dc into each of next 2 sts, 1 dc into next st, sl st into last st. (14 sts)

Fasten off leaving a long tail. Embroider eye lines to achieve a sleepy effect. Use black embroidery thread and long stitches, refer to the photograph as a guide. Embroider eye lines on to crocheted eyes before attaching on to bootie.

Tail

Using CC3.
Round 1: 6 dc into a magic loop, pull magic loop to close shut. (6 sts)

Cont to work in a spiral.

Round 2: 2 dc into each st. (12 sts)

Round 3: *2 dc into next st, 1 dc into next st; rep from * to end. (18 sts)

Round 4: *2 dc into next st, 1 dc into each of next 2 sts; rep from * to end. (24 sts)

Rounds 5–6: 1 dc into each st. (24 sts)

Round 7: *Invdec over next 2 sts, 1 dc into each of next 2 sts; rep from* to end. (18 sts)

Fill with polyester fibre filling.

Round 8: *Invdec over next 2 sts; rep from * 7 more times, 1 dc into next st, 1 sl st into last st. Fasten off leaving a tail.

Finishing

Take a long strand of CC4 and a yarn needle. Make a long horizontal stitch across the toe where you want the nose to be, and stitch over it until you have achieved the desired thickness. Make a second horizontal stitch below the first stitch and stitch over. Make third long stitch below the second stitch, keep stitching over that stitch. Now stitch over all three long stitches, covering the previous stitches for a cute and chubby nose.

19

BUZZY BEE SLIPPERS

Watch your baby buzz around in these adorable Mary-Janes. They are simple to stitch up and are sweet as honey with little wings and antennae.

BEFORE YOU BEGIN

SKILL LEVEL
1

YOU WILL NEED
Cascade 220 Sport DK 50g (1.75oz); 150m (164yds);
100% Peruvian highland wool
1 in Goldenrod (7827) = MC
1 in Charcoal Grey (8400) = CC1
Small amount of White (8505) = CC2

Hook
2.5mm for 0–6 months
3.0mm for 6–12 months
(see note, page 135)
Adjust hook size if necessary to achieve correct tension

Notions
Stitch marker
Yarn needle

TENSION
18 sts and 22 rows in dc to measure 10cm (4in)

SIZES
0–6 months, sole length 9cm (3½in)
6–12 months, sole length 10cm (4in)

Note: Instructions are given for the smallest size first; the larger size is given in square brackets [ ]

STITCHES AND SKILLS
See Crochet Basics
(pages 134–142)

Working in rows
Working in rounds
dc2tog
dc3tog

NOTE
The bootie is worked from toe to heel.
The eyes, antennae, wings and edging are the same for both sizes.

To Make the Booties

(make 2)

Sole

Using MC.

Round 1: Make 2 ch, 6 dc into 2nd ch from hook. (6 sts)

Cont to work in a spiral.

Round 2: 2 dc into each st. (12 sts)

Round 3: *1 dc into next st, 2 dc into next st; rep from * 5 more times. (18 sts)

HELPFUL TIP

When changing colours, finish last st up to the final pull through. Drop current colour, pick up next colour and finish the last pull through. Do not fasten off the dropped colour. Simply pick it up next time it is needed.

Round 4: *1 dc into each of next 2 sts, 2 dc into next st; rep from * 5 more times. (24 sts)

Rounds 5–8[10]: 1 dc into each st. (24 sts)

Round 9[11]: Join CC1, drop MC, 1 dc into each st, sl st into first dc to join. (24 sts)

Round 10[12]: 1 ch, 1 dc into each st, drop CC1, pick up MC, sl st into first dc to join. Turn.

Now work in rows.

Row 11[13]: 1 ch, 1 dc into each of next 20 sts, turn, leaving 4 sts unworked. (20 sts)

Row 12[14]: 1 ch, 1 dc into each of next 20 sts, drop MC, pick up CC1, turn. (20 sts)

Row 13[15]: 1 ch, 1 dc into each st, turn. (20 sts)

Row 14[16]: 1 ch, 1 dc into each st, drop CC1, pick up MC, turn. (20 sts)

Rows 15–16[17–18]: Rep Rows 11 and 12[13 and 14]. (20 sts)

Rows 17–18[19–20]: Rep Rows 13 and 14[15 and 16]. (20 sts)

Row 19[21]: 1 ch, 1 dc into each of next 7 sts, *dc2tog; rep from * twice more, 1 dc into each of next 7 sts, turn. (17 sts).

Row 20[22]: 1 ch, 1 dc into each of next 6 sts, dc2tog, 1 dc into next st, dc2tog, 1 dc into each of next 6 sts, turn. Fasten off MC, pick up CC1. (15 sts)

Row 21[23]: 1 ch, 1 dc into each of next 6 sts, dc3tog, 1 dc into each of next 6 sts, sl st into first stitch to join. (13 sts)

Cont to work in a spiral.

Round 22[24]: 1 ch, 1 dc into next st, *dc2tog; rep from * 5 more times, do not join. (7 sts)

Round 23[25]: 1 dc into each st. (7 sts)

Round 24[26]: 1 dc into next st, *dc2tog; rep from * twice more. (4 sts)

Round 25[27]: *Dc2tog; rep from * once more. (2 sts)

Fasten off and weave ends into WS.

Edging

Using CC1.

Round 1: Join CC1 at back centre, 1 ch, using the ends of rows as sts, 1 dc into each stitch, sl st into first dc to join.

Round 2 (make strap): 1 ch, sl st until you reach the second CC1 stripe, 6 ch, sl st to the opposite

side at the second CC1, sl st to end, sl st into the first sl st to join.

Eyes

(make 2 per bootie)

Using a yarn needle and CC1, sew eyes on to the toe of the bootie, refer to the photograph as a guide. Fasten off and weave ends into WS.

Antennae

(make 2 per bootie)

Using CC1, join yarn with a sl st to any st above eyes, 4 ch, fasten off leaving a short piece of yarn. Fray end. Secure knot. Weave ends into WS.

Wings

(make 2 per bootie)

Using CC2.

Round 1: Make 2 ch, 5 dc into 2nd ch from hook, sl st into first dc to join. (5 sts)

Round 2: 1 ch, 2 dc into each st, turn. (10 sts)

Round 3: 1 ch, dc3tog, fasten off, leaving a long tail. Using a yarn needle, sew wings on each side near the strap. Weave ends into WS.

20

SLEEPY OWLS

Twit twoo. These happy owl booties are a hoot! They are adorable in any colour, so they can match a favourite outfit or a baby shower gift.

BEFORE YOU BEGIN

SKILL LEVEL
2

YOU WILL NEED
Debbie Bliss Rialto DK 50g (1.75oz); 105m (115yds); 100% merino wool
1 in Vintage Pink (66) = MC
1 in Citrus (69) = CC1
Small amount of DK weight yarn in light grey = CC2
Small amount of DK weight yarn in brown = CC3
Small amount of DK weight yarn in green = CC4
Small amount of DK weight yarn in pale lilac= CC5
Small amount of DK weight yarn in dark lilac = CC6
Small amount of DK weight yarn in yellow = CC7

Hook
2.5mm for 0–6 months.
3.0mm for 6–12 months.
(see note, page 135)
Adjust hook size if necessary to achieve correct tension

Notions
Stitch marker
Yarn needle

TENSION
11 sts and 8 rows in htr to measure 5cm (2in) with 2.5mm hook
11 sts and 8 rows in htr to measure 5.5cm (2¼in) with 3.0mm hook

SIZES
0–6 months, sole length 9cm (3½in)
6–12 months, sole length 10cm (4in)

Note: Instructions are given for the smallest size first; the larger size is given in square brackets [ ]

STITCHES AND SKILLS
See Crochet Basics (pages 134–142)

Working in rows
Working in rounds
Working into back loops
Magic loop
Invdec

To Make the Booties

(make 2)

Sole

Using CC1.

Round 1: Make 13 ch, 1 htr into 3rd ch from hook, 1 htr into each of next 9 sts, 6 htr into last ch, working on opposite side, 1 htr into each of next 9 sts, 5 htr into last ch, sl st into first htr to join. (30 sts)

Round 2: 1 ch, 1 htr into each of next 10 sts, 2 htr into each of next 5 sts, 1 htr into each of next 10 sts, 2 htr into each of next 5 sts, sl st into first htr to join. (40 sts)

To care for these booties, hand-wash in cold water and air dry, do not wring.

Round 3: 1 ch, 1 htr into each of next 10 sts, *2 htr into next st, 1 htr into next st*; rep from * to * 4 more times, 1 htr into each of next 10 sts, rep from * to * 5 more times, sl st into first htr to join. (50 sts)

Change to CC1 and cont with upper.

Upper

Using MC.
Round 1: 1 dc blo into each of next 50 sts, sl st into first dc to join.

Rounds 2–5: 1 ch, 1 dc into each st, sl st into first dc to join.

Note: After first 1 ch, work first dc into same st. The first 1 ch does not count as a st.

Round 6: 1 ch, 1 dc into same st, *Invdec over next 2 sts, 1 dc into next st; rep from * 9 more times, 1 dc into each of next 9 sts, Invdec over next 2 sts, 1 dc into each of next 7 sts, sl st into first dc to join. (38 sts)

Round 7: 1 ch, 1 dc into each st, sl st into first dc to join. (38 sts)

Round 8: 1 ch, 1 dc into same st, 1 dc into each of next 6 sts, *Invdec over next 2 sts; rep from * 3 more times, 1 dc into each of next 13 sts, Invdec over next 2 sts, 1 dc into next st, Invdec over next 2 sts, 1 dc into each of next 5 sts, sl st into first dc to join. (32 sts) Fasten off.

Eyes

(make 2 per bootie)

Using CC2.
Round 1: 6 dc into a magic loop, pull magic loop to close shut. (6 sc)

Cont to work in a spiral.

Round 2: 2 dc into each of next 2 sts, 1 dc into each of next 2 sts, 2 dc into each of next 2 sts. (10 sts)

Round 3: 1 dc into each of next 2 sts, 2 dc into each of next 2 sts, 1 dc into each of next 2 sts, 2 dc into each of next 2 sts, 1 dc into next st, 1 sl st into next st. (14 sts)

Fasten off leaving a long tail. Using CC3, embroider eye lines to create a sleepy effect, refer to the photograph as a guide. Embroider eye lines to crocheted eyes before attaching on to the bootie. Make a knot with CC4 as follows: take two long yarn strands and pull through the last row of the eye, then make a knot and trim the ends into a tassel.

Wings

(make 2 per bootie)

Using CC5.
Round 1: 6 dc into a magic loop, pull magic loop to close shut. (6 sts)

Cont to work in a spiral.

Round 2: 2 dc into first st, 1 dc into each of next 2 sts, 2 dc into next st, 1 dc into each of next 2 sts. (8 sts)

Round 3: 2 dc into first st, 4 dtr into next st, 1 dc into each of next 2 sts, 2 dc into each of next 3 sts, sl st into last st. (15 sts)

Fasten off leaving a long tail. Attach the rounded half of the wing to the side of the shoe, leaving the pointed end free.

Tail

Using CC6 and leaving a long tail at beg.
Round 1: 6 dc into a magic loop, pull magic loop to close shut. (6 sts)

Cont to work in a spiral.

Round 2: 2 dc into each st. (12 sts)

Round 3: *2 dc into first st, 1 dc into next st, rep from * to end. (18 sts)

Round 4: 1 dc into each st. (18 sts)

Fold the tail together, join the top edges together by working under blo to create a ridge, work 1 dc into each of next 8 sts. For best results, make one more dc at the end of the row to create a nice neat tail for both sides. Fasten off and weave ends into WS.

Beak

Using CC7.
Row 1: 4 ch, 1 dc into the 2nd ch from hook, 1 dc into each of next 2 sts, turn. (3 sts)

Rows 2–4: 1 ch, 1 dc into each st, turn. (3 sts)

Row 5: 1 ch, skip 1 st, 1 dc into each of last 2 sts, turn. (2 sts)

Row 6: 1 ch, skip 1 st, 1 dc into last st. (1 st)

Fasten off leaving a long tail.

Finishing

Sew the beak to front of the bootie. Attach the tail to the back of the bootie, using the tail ends of the yarn. Weave ends into WS.

21 FOXY FEET

Crocheted in two pieces and sewn together, these booties are moccasin-style slippers with a foxy little face. A quirky finish to any outfit.

BEFORE YOU BEGIN

SKILL LEVEL
2

YOU WILL NEED
Cascade 220 Sport 50g (1.75oz); 150m (164yds); 100% Peruvian highland wool
1 in Ginger (2414) = MC
1 in Natural (8010) = CC1
Small amount of aran weight yarn in black= CC2

Hook
3.75mm (US F/5)
Adjust hook size if necessary to achieve correct tension

Notions
Yarn needle

TENSION
11 sts and 8 rows in htr to measure 5cm (2in)

SIZES
0–6 months, sole length 9cm (3½in)
6–12 months, sole length 10cm (4in)

Note: Instructions are given for the smallest size first; the larger size is given in square brackets [ ]

STITCHES AND SKILLS
See Crochet Basics (pages 134–142)

Sole 1
Working in rows
Working in rounds
Working into front and back loops
Magic loop
dc3tog
htr3tog

To Make the Booties

(make 2)

Face

Using CC1.
Row 1: Make 12 ch, 2 dc into 2nd ch from hook, 1 dc into each of next 3 ch, dc3tog across next 3 ch, 1 dc into each of next 3 ch, 2 dc into last ch, turn. (11 sts)

Row 2: 1 ch, 2 dc into first st, 1 dc into each of next 3 sts, dc3tog across next 3 sts, 1 dc into each of next 3 sts, 2 dc into last st, switching to MC during last dc, turn. (11 sts)

Cut CC1, leaving a 120cm (48in) tail to work with later. Work over this tail with next row.

Row 3–6: 1 ch, 2 dc into first st, 1 dc into each of next 3 sts, dc3tog across next 3 sts, 1 dc into each of next 3 sts, 2 dc into last st, turn. (11 sts)

Row 7: Working around entire piece, 1 ch, (1 dc, 2 ch, 1 dc) into first st, 1 dc into each of next 3 sts, dc3tog across next 3 sts, 1 dc into each of next 3 sts, (1 dc, 2 ch, 1 dc) into last st. Rotate piece clockwise: work 1 dc into side of each of the 5 rows to the foundation chain, switching to CC1 when you reach the CC1 rows, working over MC tail. Rotate piece clockwise to work on opposite side of foundation chain: 3 dc into first st, 1 dc into each of next 4 sts, (1 dc, 1 ch, 1 dc) into next st, 1 dc into each of next 4 sts, 3 dc into last st. Rotate piece clockwise: 5 dc up the final side, switching back to MC when appropriate, sl st into first dc to join. Fasten off.

Use CC1 to embroider a V shape into each ear.

Nose

Using CC2.

Round 1: 6 dc into a magic loop, pull magic loop to close shut, sl st into first dc to join. (6 sts)

Fasten off, leaving an approx 90cm (36in) tail to sew the nose in place on the face (do not sew over the edge of face). Embroider eyes with CC2 before proceeding to sole.

Sole

Work Sole 1, ending with 46[50] sts.

Round 4: 1 ch, 1 htr blo into each st, including st at the join, sl st into first htr to join. (46[50] htr)

Round 5: 1 ch, 1 htr into same space and 1 htr into each st around, sl st into first htr to join. (46[50] htr)

HELPFUL TIP

If the opening of the bootie is too loose, or baby's feet are smaller than average, join the top edges of the cuff before sewing them behind the face.

Fasten off, weave ends into WS. Mark the centre front and back of slipper bottom, with 22[24] stitches between each marker. Using MC, attach the face to the slipper bottom, starting at the tip of the nose to the 3rd st from the tip of the ear (approx 11[12] sts), rep for other side of face. The ears should be able to move freely.

Back

Using MC.

Note: Slipper back is worked over the back 23[25] sts. Count 11[12] sts from centre back and re-attach MC.

Row 1: 1 ch, 1 htr into same sp, 1 htr into each of next 9[10] sts, htr3tog across next 3 sts, 1 htr into each of next 10[11] sts, turn. (21[23] htr)

Row 2–7: 1 ch, 1 htr into each st, turn. (21[23] htr)

Fasten off, leaving a long tail end. Fold the cuff down and use tail to sew it down to top of Row 2. Use same tail, or another scrap of MC, to sew the front tips of the cuff to the back of the face, at the sts directly to the left and right of centre st between the ears.

Finishing

Weave ends into WS. Lightly block, if desired.

22

SPLASH AROUND

HELPFUL TIP

Make sure that the little fins and tail fins are securely fastened to the main body of the bootie. Attach the fins using leftover yarn in MC.

These bright and cheerful goldfish booties will have those little legs swimming away with the help of the frilly fins and tail.

BEFORE YOU BEGIN

SKILL LEVEL
2

YOU WILL NEED
Debbie Bliss Rialto DK 50g (1.75oz); 105m (115yds); 100% merino wool
1 in Coral (55) = MC
Small amount of White (01) = CC1
Small amount of Black (03) = CC2
Small amount of Apple (09) = CC3

Hook
2.5mm (see note, page 135)
Adjust hook size if necessary to achieve correct tension

Notions
Stitch marker
Yarn needle

TENSION
11 sts and 8 rows in htr to measure 5cm (2in)

SIZES
0–6 months, sole length 9cm (3½in)
6–12 months, sole length 10cm (4in)

Note: Instructions are given for the smallest size first; the larger size is given in square brackets [ ]

STITCHES AND SKILLS
See Crochet Basics (pages 134–142)

Working in rounds
Working into front and back loops
Magic loop
Invdec
dc2tog

NOTES
The booties are crocheted in the round. Do not join the rounds.

To Make the Booties

(make 2)

Body

Using MC.
Round 1: 6 dc into a magic loop, pull magic loop to close shut.(6 sts)

Cont to work in a spiral.

Round 2: 2 dc into each st. (12 sts)

Rounds 3–4: 1 dc into each st. (12 sts)

Round 5: 2 dc into each of next 2 sts, 1 dc into each of next 2 sts, 2 dc into each of next 4 sts, 1 dc into each of next 2 sts, 2 dc into each of next 2 sts. (20 sts)

Round 6: 2 dc into each of next 3 sts, 1 dc into each of next 4 sts, 2 dc into each of next 6 sts,

1 dc into each of next 4 sts, 2 dc into each of next 3 sts. (32 sts)

Round 7: 1 dc into each of next 2 sts, *2 dc into next st, 1 dc into next st; rep from * 4 more times, 1 dc into each of next 20 sts. (37 sts)

Round 8: 1 dc into each st. (37 sts)

Round 9: 1 dc into each of next 2 sts, *2 dc into next st, 1 dc into each of next 2 sts; rep from * 4 more times, 1 dc into each of next 20 sts. (42 sts)

Rounds 10–12: 1 dc into each st. (42 sts)

Round 13: 1 dc into each of next 2 sts, *Invdec over next 2 sts, 1 dc into each of next 2 sts; rep from * 4 more times, 1 dc into each of next 20 sts. (37 sts)

Round 14: 1 dc into each st. (37 sts)

Round 15: 1 dc into each of next 2 sts, *Invdec over next 2 sts, 1 dc into next st; rep from * 4 more times, 1 dc into each of next 20 sts. (32 sts)

Rounds 16–17: 1 dc into each st. (32 sts)

For larger size only: Rep Rounds 16–17 once more.

Round 18[20]: 1 dc into each of next 4 sts, turn.

Cont to work in rows.

Row 19[21]: 1 ch (not counted as a st), 1 dc into each of next 24 sts, turn.

Row 20[22]–27[29]: Rep Round 19[21] 8 more times.

Row 28[30]: 1 ch, 1 dc into each of next 9 sts, dc2tog 3 times over next 6 sts, 1 dc into each of next 9 sts, turn. (21 sts)

Row 29[31]: 1 ch, 1 dc into each of next 6 sts, dc2tog, 1 dc into each of next 5 sts, dc2tog, 1 dc into each of next 6 sts, turn. (19 sts)

Row 30[32]: 1 ch, 1 dc into each of next 6 sts, dc2tog, 1 dc into each of next 3 sts, dc2tog, 1 dc into each of next 6 sts, turn. (17 sts)

Cont with edging as follows: work around all 3 sides of the bootie with dc, working l dc into each row end and each st.

Join back seam as follows: fold WS together and join first 4 sts with dc under both loops of each set of sts, then cont with sl st under two middle loops only into last sts. Fasten off.

Tail Fin

Leave a tail of yarn for sewing before making the magic loop.

Using MC.
Round 1: 6 dc into a magic loop, pull magic loop to close shut. (6 sts)

Cont to work in a spiral.

Round 2: 2 dc into each st. (12 sts)

Round 3: *2 dc into next st, 1 dc into next st; rep from * to end. (18 sts)

Round 4: *2 dc into next st, 1 dc into each of next 2 sts; rep from * to end. (24 sts)

Next, fold the fin and join the top edges together by working into blo to create a ridge on the front of the fin, making a row with dc, into each of next 11 sts. For best results, make one more dc at the end of the row to create a nice neat fin for both sides. Fasten off and weave ends to WS. Cont with CC1.

Round 5: 1 dc into first st, 6 htr into next st, 1 dc into each of next 3 sts, 6 htr into next st, 1 dc into each of next 3 sts, 6 htr into next st, 1 dc into last st. (26 sts)

Round 6: 1 dc into each of next 12 sts, 6 htr into next st, 1 dc into each of next 12 sts. (30 sts)

Round 7: 1 dc into each of next 3 sts, 6 htr into next st, 1 dc into each of next 10 sts, 6 htr into next st, 1 dc into each of next 10 sts, 6 htr into next st, 1 dc into each of next 3 sts, sl st at the end of the row. Fasten off and weave ends into WS.

Little Fins

(make 2 per bootie)

Leave a tail of yarn for sewing before making the magic loop.

Using MC.
Round 1: 6 dc into a magic loop, pull magic loop to close shut. (6 sts)

Cont to work in a spiral.

Round 2: 2 dc into each st. (12 sts)

Round 3: *2 dc into next st, 1 dc into next st; rep from * to end. (18 sts)

Next, fold the fin and join the top edges together by working into blo to create a ridge on the front of the fin, making a row with dc, into each of next 8 sts. For best results, make one more dc at the end of the row to create a nice neat fin for both sides. Fasten off and weave ends into WS. Cont with CC1.

Round 4: 3 dc into next st, 1 dc into each of next 2 sts, 5 htr into next st, 5 htr into next st, 1 dc into each of next 2 sts, 3 dc into next st. Fasten off and weave ends into WS.

Eyes

(make 2 per bootie)

Using CC2.
Round 1: 6 dc into a magic loop, pull magic loop to close shut. (6 sts)

Switch to CC3 and cont to work in a spiral.

Round 2: 2 dc into each st. (12 sts)

Switch to MC.

Round 3: 1 dc into each of next 11 sts, 1 sl st into last st. Fasten off, leaving a tail end.

Finishing

Sew the eyes to each side of bootie using tail end. Sew the tail fin to the back of bootie and the little fins to the side of bootie, using the photograph as a guide. Flatten the upper side of the bootie together to form a fin on the head of the fish, and sew both parts together with small sts using MC.

23

STARFISH SANDALS

Perfect for summer days, these sandals will delight your little one with their bright starfish decoration. An open back with sandal straps makes for cooler tootsies when the temperature begins to creep up.

BEFORE YOU BEGIN

SKILL LEVEL
1

YOU WILL NEED
Debbie Bliss Mia 50g (1.75oz); 100m (109ydsm); 50% cotton/ 50% wool
1 in Sky (04) = MC
1 in Corn (14) = CC1
1 in Rose (10) = CC2

Hook
3.5mm (US E/4)
Adjust hook size if necessary to achieve correct tension

Notions
Stitch marker
Yarn needle

TENSION
9 sts and 11 rows in dc to measure 5cm (2in)

SIZES
0–6 months, sole length 9cm (3½in)
6–12 months, sole length 10cm (4in)

Note: Instructions are given for the smallest size first; the larger size is given in square brackets [ ]

STITCHES AND SKILLS
See Crochet Basics (pages 134–142)

Sole 2
Working in rows
Working in rounds
Working into front and back loops
Magic loop
dc2tog
tr2tog
tr6tog

To Make the Booties

(make 2)

Sole

Make one of each of Sole 2 in MC and CC1 per bootie. Sew the soles together using a yarn needle and CC1.

Toe Section

Locate the 2 centre sts of the toe, count 10 sts to the left.

Row 1: Join MC into the 10th st of MC sole, 1 ch, 1 dc blo into each of next 20 sts, turn. (20 sts)

Row 2: 1 ch, 1 dc into each of next 6 sts, *tr2tog; rep from * 3 more times, 1 dc into each of next 6 sts, turn. (16 sts)

Row 3: 1 ch, 1 dc into each of next 4 sts, *tr2tog; rep from * 3 more times, 1 dc into each of next 4 sts, turn. (12 sts)

Row 4: 1 ch, 1 dc into each of next 2 sts, *tr2tog; rep from * 4 more times, 1 dc into each of next 2 sts, turn. (8 sts)

Row 5: 2 ch, tr6tog, 2 ch, sl st into last st.

Fasten off. Weave in ends in WS.

Heel Strap Support

Using MC.
Locate the two centre sts of the heel.

Row 1: Join MC into the right centre st of MC sole, 1 ch, 1 dc into each of next 2 sts, turn. (2 sts)

Rows 2–10: 1 ch, 1 dc into each of next 2 sts, turn. Fasten off, leaving a long tail.

Fold the strip over, and use a yarn needle to sew into place.

Strap

Using MC.

Row 1: Make 21[25] ch, turn, 1 htr into 2nd ch from hook, 1 htr into each rem ch. (20[24] sts)

Fasten off. Using a yarn needle, sew each strap on to the toe section on Rows 2 and 3, making sure you feed the strap through the heel strap support.

Star

Using CC2.
Round 1: 2 ch, 5 dc into 2nd ch from hook, sl st into first dc to join. (5 sts)

Round 2: 1 ch, 1 dc into same st, 5 ch, 1 dc into 2nd ch from hook, 1 dc into each of next 3 ch, 1 dc into same st at base of 5 ch, *1 dc into next st, 5 ch, 1 dc into 2nd ch from hook, 1 dc into each of next 3 ch, 1 dc into same st at base of 5 ch; rep from * 3 more times, sl st into first ch to join.

Round 3: 1 ch, *dc2tog, 1 dc into each of next 3 sts, 2 dc into next st, 1 dc into each of next 2 sts, dc2tog; rep from * 4 more times, sl st into first st to join. Fasten off. Weave ends into WS.

Using a yarn needle and CC1, stitch around the last row of the star until it is completely outlined. Fasten off. Weave ends into WS.

Finishing

Using CC2, sew the star on to the toe section making sure it is securely attached.

HELPFUL TIP
You can add any appliqué to the top of these pretty sandals – strawberries would be a cute choice.

GOOD ENOUGH TO EAT

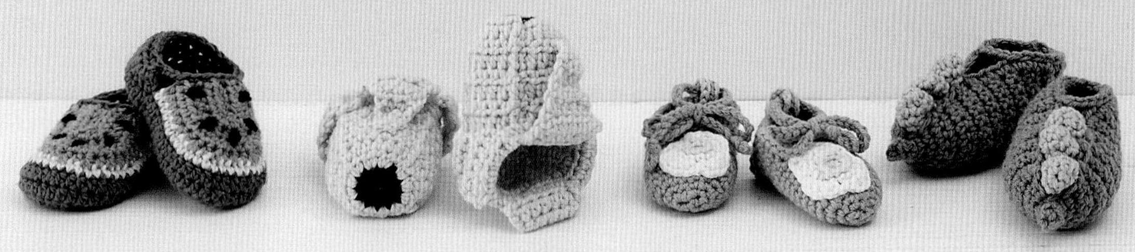

24

SWEET FEET

Uniquely constructed with a spiralling swirl of ice cream, these sweet booties are really easy to make. They are sugar-free, leave no crumbs and are sure to make you smile.

BEFORE YOU BEGIN

SKILL LEVEL
2

YOU WILL NEED
Cascade 220 Sport 50g (1.75oz); 150m (164yds); 100% Peruvian highland wool
1 in White (8505) = MC
1 in Beige (8021) = CC1
Small amount of DK weight yarn in cherry red = CC2
Random-coloured scraps for sprinkles

Hook
3.75mm (US F/5)
Adjust hook size if necessary to achieve correct tension

Notions
Stitch marker
Yarn needle

TENSION
11 sts and 8 rows in htr to measure 5cm (2in)

SIZES
0–6 months, sole length 9cm (3½in)
6–12 months, sole length 10cm (4in)

Note: Instructions are given for the smallest size first; the larger size is given in square brackets [ ]

STITCHES AND SKILLS
See Crochet Basics (pages 134–142)

Working in rows
Working in rounds
Working into front and back loops
Magic loop
slst2tog
fptr
dc2tog

NOTE
Starting from Round 2 of cone bottom, 3 ch at beginning counts as 1 tr st.

To Make the Booties

(make 2)

Ice Cream Top

Using MC.
Work all rows into blo.

Row 1: Make 15[17] ch, 1 dc into 2nd ch from hook, 1 dc into each of next 10[12] ch, sl st into each of next 3 ch, turn. (14[16] sts)

Row 2: 1 ch, slst2tog, sl st into each of next 2 sts, 1 dc into each of next 9[11] sts, 2 dc into next st, turn. (14[16] sts)

Row 3: 1 ch, 2 dc into first st, 1 dc into each of next 9[11] sts, sl st into each of next 2 sts, slst2tog, turn. (14[16] sts)

Rep Rows 2–3 7[8] more times, rep Row 2 once more. Do not fasten off.

The last row is the right side (RS). Embroider sprinkles with random-coloured scraps of yarn onto RS (see tip, opposite), then turn (do not work 1 ch). With WS facing, bring foundation row up, WS together, working in flo of side closest to you and blo of side farthest away, sl st the final row to the foundation row. Fasten off, leaving a tail of approx 90cm (36in). Use the yarn tail to close the sl st edge shut. This is the top of the ice cream. The rest of the bootie will be worked from the bottom edge. Weave ends into WS.

Cone

Being mindful of the seam, attach MC to bottom edge of the ice cream, at approx 5 rows to the right of the seam.

Round 1: 1 ch, work 20[22] dc into sides of ice cream bottom, sl st into first dc to join, switching to CC1.

Round 2: 3 ch, 1 tr into flo of next st, 1 tr into flo of each rem st, sl st into top of beg 3 ch. (20[22] sts)

Round 3: 1 ch, 1 htr into same st and into corresponding back loop of round 1 (the joining st), *1 htr into next st of Round 2 and into corresponding back loop of Round 1; rep from * to end. (20[22] sts)

Cont to work in rows.

Row 4: 1 ch, 1 htr into each of first 16[17] sts, leaving last 4[5] sts unworked, turn. (16[17] sts)

Row 5: 1 ch, 1 htr into each st, turn. (16[17] sts)

Row 6: 1 ch, 1 htr into first st, 1 fptr around next st of Round 4, 1 htr into each of next 3 sts, 1 fptr around next st of Round 4, 1 htr into each of next 4[5] sts, 1 fptr around next st of Round 4, 1 htr into each of next 3 sts, 1 fptr around next st of Round 4, 1 htr into last st, turn. (16[17] sts)

Row 7–9[10]: Rep rows 5–6, making the fptr sts around each other, ending with Row 5[6].

Next Row: 1 ch, 1 dc into each of next 6[7] sts along edge of rows, 1 dc into each of next 4[5] unworked sts of Round 3, 1 dc into each of next 6[7] sts along other edge, sl st into first dc to join.

Fasten off, leaving a tail of approx 45cm (18in). Fold last row in half and seam edge together. Weave ends into WS.

Cherry

Using CC2.

Round 1: 6 dc into a magic loop, pull magic loop to close shut. (6 dc)

Cont to work in a spiral.

Round 2: *1 dc into next st, 2 dc into next st; rep from * twice more. (9 sts)

Round 3: *1 dc into next st, dc2tog; rep from * twice more, sl st into first dc to join. (6 sts)

Cut yarn, leaving a tail of approx 45cm (18in). Weave tail through sts to close the gap.

Finishing

Sew the cherry to the tip of the ice cream using tail end of yarn. When secure, thread yarn end through the top of the cherry to create a stem.

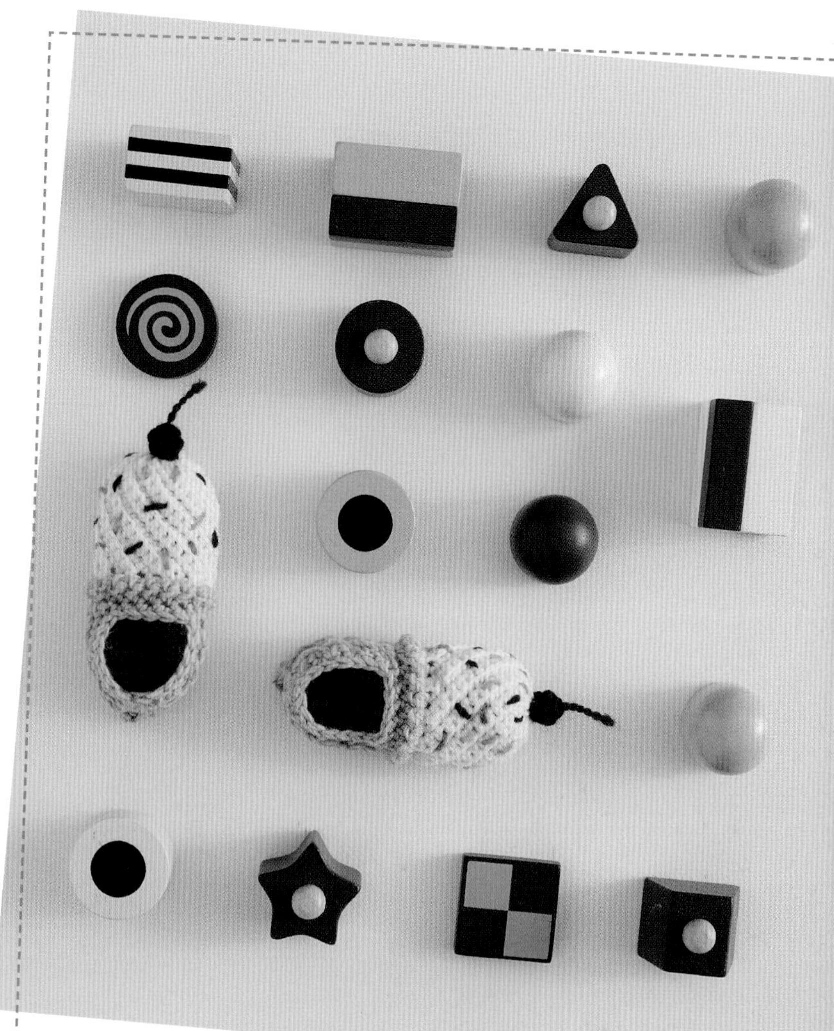

HELPFUL TIP

Simple sprinkles can be made with about 4cm (1½in) of yarn, knotted on the inside of the bootie.

25
BURGER
BOOTIES

Order a side of fries and a milkshake with these quirky hamburger booties – yummier than any take-away. With chunky layers of burger, bun, lettuce, tomato and cheese, they are not just fun to look at, they are fun to wear too.

BEFORE YOU BEGIN

SKILL LEVEL
3

YOU WILL NEED
Debbie Bliss Rialto DK 50g (1.75oz); 105m (115yds); 100% merino wool
1 in Camel (67) = MC
Small amount of Jade (71) = CC1
Small amount of Chocolate (05) = CC2
Small amount of Banana (57) = CC3
Small amount of Scarlet (12) = CC4
Small amount of white yarn = CC5

Hook
3.25mm (US D/3)
Adjust hook size if necessary to achieve correct tension

Notions
Stitch marker
Yarn needle

TENSION
11 sts and 12 rows in dc to measure 5cm (2in)

SIZES
0–6 months, sole length 9cm (3½in)
6–12 months, sole length 10cm (4in)

Note: Instructions are given for the smallest size first; the larger size is given in square brackets [ ]

STITCHES AND SKILLS
See Crochet Basics (pages 134–142)

Working in rounds
Working into front and back loops
Magic loop
dc2tog
htr2tog

NOTES
CC1 yarn used in photographs is Grass (58), discontinued.
Pattern is worked in rounds. Do not turn at the end of a round.
Join each round with a sl st into first st.
First 1 ch does not count as st.

To Make the Booties

(make 2)

Bottom Bun

Using MC.
Round 1: 6 dc into a magic loop, pull magic loop to close shut, sl st into first dc to join. (6 sts)

Round 2: 1 ch, 2 dc into each st. (12sts)

Round 3: 1 ch, *2 dc into next st, 1 dc into next st; rep from * 5 more times. (18 sts)

Round 4: 1 ch, *2 dc into next st, 1 dc into each of next 2 sts; rep from * 5 more times. (24 sts)

Round 5: 1 ch, *2 dc into next st, 1 dc into each of next 3 sts; rep from * 5 more times. (30 sts)

Round 6: 1 ch, *2 dc into next st, 1 dc into each of next 4 sts; rep from * 5 more times. (36 sts)

Round 7: 1 ch, *2 dc into next st, 1 dc into each of next 5 sts; rep from * 5 more times. (42 sts)

Round 8: 1 ch, *2 dc into next st, 1 dc into each of next 6 sts; rep from * 5 more times. (48 sts)

For larger size only: Round 9: 1 ch, *2 dc into next st, 1 dc into each of next 7 sts; rep from * 5 more times. ([54 sts])

Round 9[10]: 1 ch, 1 dc blo into each st. (54 sts)

Round 10[11]: 1 ch, working under both loops, *dc2tog, 1 dc into each of next 6[7] sts; rep from * 5 more times, switch to CC1. (42[48] sts)

Burger Fillings

Round 1: 1 ch, *2 dc flo into next st, 3 dc flo into next st; rep from * to end.

Insert hook into back loop of Round 10[11] from bottom bun and switch to CC2.

Round 2: 1 ch, working into back loops of Round 10[11] from bottom bun, 1 dc into each st, sl st into first dc to join. (42[48] sts)

HELPFUL TIP

Embroider sesame seeds on to the top third of the burger bun. Space at random intervals, using the photograph as a guide.

Round 3: 1 ch, *2 dc into next st, 1 dc into each of next 6[7] sts; rep from * 5 more times, insert hook into flo of first st and switch to CC3. (48[54] sts)

Round 4 (work in flo): 1 ch, *sl st into each of next 9[10] sts, 1 htr into next st, [2 htr, 2 ch, 2 htr] into next st; 1 htr into next st, sl st into each of next 9[11] sts, 1 htr into next st, [2 htr, 2 ch, 2 htr] into next st, 1 htr into next st; rep from * once more, insert hook into back loop of Round 3 and switch to CC4.

Round 5: 1 ch, working in blo from Round 3, 1 htr into each st, insert hook into first st and switch to MC for top bun. (48[54] sts)

Round 6 (work in flo): 1 ch, *2 dc into next st, 1 dc into each of next 7[8] sts; rep from * 5 more times, sl st into first st to join. (54[60] sts)

Rounds 7–8: 1 ch, 1 dc into each st.

Round 9: 1 ch, *dc2tog, 1 dc into each of next 7[8] sts; rep from * 5 more times. (48[54] sts)

For larger size only: Round 10: 1 ch, *dc2tog, 1 dc into each of next 7 sts; rep from * 5 more times. (48sts)

Round 10[11]: 1 ch, 1 dc into next st, dc2tog, 1 dc into each of next 6 sts, *1 htr into next st, htr2tog; rep from * 5 more times, 1 dc into each of next 7 sts, **dc2tog, 1 dc into next st; rep from ** 3 more times, dc2tog. (36sts)

Round 11[12]: 1 ch, 1 dc into each of next 7 sts, *htr2tog, 1 htr into next st; rep from *4 more times, 1 dc into each of next 14 sts. (31 sts)

Round 12[13]: 1 ch, 1 dc into each of next 8 sts, *htr2tog; rep from *4 more times, 1 dc into each of next 13 sts. Fasten off and weave ends into WS.

Finishing

Using CC5 and a yarn needle, embroider sesame seeds on to the top bun. Weave ends into WS.

26 BANANA SLIPPERS

Slip these banana skins on your baby's feet. These quirky booties may not count as one of your five-a-day, but they make up for it in their cuteness. The perfect accessory for any little monkey.

BEFORE YOU BEGIN

SKILL LEVEL
2

YOU WILL NEED
Debbie Bliss Rialto DK 50g (1.75oz); 105m (115yds); 100% merino wool
1 in Banana (57) = MC
Small amount of Chocolate (05) = CC1

Hook
3.25mm (US D/3)
Adjust hook size if necessary to achieve correct tension

Notions
4 stitch markers
Yarn needle

TENSION
10 sts and 8 rows in htr to measure 5cm (2in)

SIZES
0–6 months, sole length 9cm (3½in)
6–12 months, sole length 10cm (4in)

Note: Instructions are given for the smallest size first; the larger size is given in square brackets [ ]

STITCHES AND SKILLS
See Crochet Basics (pages 134–142)

Working in rows
Working in rounds
Magic loop
fphtr
bphtr
htr2tog

NOTE
Make first st(s) into same st as sl st join.
Foot is worked in rounds using toe-up technique. For the foot, first 1 ch does not count as st.

To Make the Booties

(make 2)

Foot

Round 1: Using CC1, 2 ch and 12 htr into a magic loop, pull magic loop to close shut, sl st into first htr to join. (12 sts)

Switch to MC, turn.

Round 2: 1 ch, 2 htr into each st, sl st into first htr to join, turn. (24 sts)

HELPFUL TIPS

Securely sewing down each of the peel segments will make a safer shoe for active babies. You can also add a non-slip sole by sewing pieces of elastic or trim to the sole.

Round 3: 1 ch, *1 htr into each of next 5 sts, 1 bphtr into next st; rep from * to end, sl st into first htr to join, turn.

Round 4: 1 ch, *1 fphtr into next st, 1 htr into each of next 5 sts; rep from * to end, sl st into first htr to join, turn.

Rep Rounds 3 and 4 2[3] more times.

Rep Round 3, turn.

Heel

Round 1: 2 ch, 1 htr into each of next 4 sts, 1 fphtr into next st, 1 htr into each of next 5 sts, 1 fphtr into next st, 1 htr into each of next 5 sts, leave rem sts unworked, turn. (17 sts)

Round 2: 2 ch, 1 htr into each of next 4 sts, *1 bphtr into next st, 1 htr into each of next 5 sts; rep from * once more, turn. (17 sts)

For larger size only: Rep Rounds 1 and 2 once more.

Round 3[5]: 2 ch, 1 htr into each of next 4 sts, htr2tog, *1 htr into next st, htr2tog; rep from * once more, 1 htr into each of next 4 sts, turn. (14 sts)

Round 4[6]: 2 ch, 1 htr into each of next 2 sts, htr2tog, 1 htr into next st, htr2tog, 1 htr into next st, htr2tog, 1 htr into each of next 3 sts, turn. (11 sts)

Round 5[7]: 2 ch, *1 htr into each of next 3 sts, htr2tog; rep from * once more, 1 htr into each of next 3 sts, sl st into top of 2 ch to join back of heel. (9 sts)

Ankle Edging

Using MC.
Hold the slipper with the toe pointing down and the sole facing you.

2 ch and evenly make 10[12] htr along the side rows, make 6 dc in rem sts from Round 3 of foot portion, evenly make 10[12] htr along the side rows, sl st to first htr. (26[30] sts)

Fasten off and leave tail to sew back seam.

Peel Segments

Using MC.
Hold the slipper with the toe pointing down and foot opening facing you, place a marker in bottom right corner of the opening. Then, moving clockwise, count 7 sts and place another marker. Continue clockwise, count 6[8]sts and place a third marker, count a further 7 sts and place a fourth marker.

Row 1: Starting with first marker, work 1 htr into same st as marker, 1 htr into each st across until st before next marker, turn.

Row 2: 2 ch, 1 htr into each st, turn.

Row 3: 2 ch, htr2tog over first 2 sts, 1 htr into each st until last 2 sts, htr2tog, turn.

Row 4: 2 ch, 1 htr into each st, turn.

Rep Rows 3 and 4 until 2 sts rem, working only 1 decrease on last row for segments with an odd number of sts. Fasten off and leave tail to sew the segment to the top of the main foot, or leave it unattached if you prefer. *Work 1 htr into same st as next marker and rep from Row 1 to end. Rep from * until there are a total of 4 peel segments.

HELPFUL TIP

For the heel, first 2 ch counts as first htr. Do not make first st(s) into same space as sl st, instead make first st into next st.

27

EGGS AND BACON

How do you like your eggs in the morning? Cover your little one's feet in these tasty treats. A cooked breakfast has never looked more delicious.

BEFORE YOU BEGIN

SKILL LEVEL
2

YOU WILL NEED
Debbie Bliss Mia DK 50g (1.75oz); 100m (109yds); 50% cotton/ 50% wool
1 in Aqua (17) = MC
Small amount of Buttermilk (19) = CC1
Small amount of White (01) = CC2
Small amount of Light Pink (11) = CC3
Small amount of Petal (20) = CC4

Hook
4mm (US G/6)
Adjust hook size if necessary to achieve correct tension

Notions
Stitch marker
Yarn needle

TENSION
20 sts and 22 rows in dc to measure 10cm (4in)

SIZES
0–6 months, sole length 9cm (3½in)
6–12 months, sole length 10cm (4in)

Note: Instructions are given for the smallest size first; the larger size is given in square brackets [ ]

STITCHES AND SKILLS
See Crochet Basics (pages 134–142)

Working in rows
Working in rounds
Working into front and back loops
Magic loop
dc2tog

To Make the Booties

(make 2)

Toe

Using MC.

Round 1: Make 3[4] ch, 2 dc into 2nd ch from hook, 1 dc into next 0[1] ch, 4 dc into last ch, working into opposite side of ch, 1 dc into next 0[1] ch, 2 dc into ch that already contains 2 dc. (8[10] sts)

Cont to work in a spiral.

Round 2: 2 dc into next st, 1 dc into each of next 2[3] sts, 2 dc into each of next 2 sts, 1 dc into each of next 2[3] sts, 2 dc into last st. (12[14] sts)

HELPFUL TIP

To make sure the ties don't come loose from the bootie, use a tack stitch to secure the centre of the tie to the bacon loop.

Round 3: 2 dc into next st , 1 dc into each of next 4[5] sts, 2 dc into each of next 2 sts, 1 dc into each of next 4[5] sts, 2 dc into last st. (16[18] sts)

Round 4: 2 dc into each of first 2 sts, 1 dc into each of next 6[7] sts, 2 dc into each of next 2 sts, 1 dc into each of next 6[7] sts. (20[22] sts)

Round 5: 1 dc into each st. (20[22] sts)

Rounds 6–10[11]: Rep Round 5. (20[22] sts)

Body

Cont in MC.
Row 1: 1 dc into each of next 16[17] sts, turn, leaving rem 4[5] sts unworked. (16[17] sts)

Cont to work in rows.

Row 2: 1 ch, 1 dc into each of next 15[16] sts, leaving rem st unworked, turn. (15[16] sts)

Row 3: 1 ch, 1 dc into each st, turn. (15[16] sts)

Row 4–11: Rep Row 3. (15[16] sts)

For larger size only: Rep Row 3 twice more. ([16] sts)

Back Seam

Fold the back seam in half with RS together. Working through flo of the piece closest to you and blo of the piece farthest away from you, join the two sides together by working a sl st though both layers into each of the next 7[8] sts.
Fasten off and weave ends into WS.

Edging Rows

Using MC.
Round 1: With RS facing, work 26[31] dc evenly around the foot opening, working 1 dc into each row end and each st, sl st into first dc to join. (26[31] sts)

For larger size only: Work 1 more round of 1 dc into each st. ([31] sts)

Fasten off and weave ends into WS.

Egg

Using CC1.
Round 1: 1 ch and 9 htr into a magic loop, pull magic loop to close shut, sl st into first htr to join. (9 sts)

Switch to CC2, work Round 2 into the third loop of each htr which lies behind the front and back loops on the WS.

Round 2: 1 ch, 2 dc into same st, 1 dc into next st, *2 dc into next st, 1 dc into next st; rep from * twice more, 2 dc into next st, sl st into first dc to join. (14 sts)

Round 3: Sl st into next st, (1 dc, 1 htr) into next st, 2 tr into next st, (1 htr, 1 dc) into next st, sl st into next st, (1 dc, 1 htr) into next st, (1 htr, 1 dc) into next st, sl st into next st, 1 dc into next st, 2 htr into next st, 1 dc into next st, sl st into each of last 2 sts. Fasten off, leaving a tail of approx 20cm (8in). (19 sts, including sl sts)

Bacon

Using CC3.

Row 1: Make 10 ch. Fasten off, leaving a tail of approx 15cm (6in). (10 sts)

Switch to CC4.

Row 2: Starting in the first ch, make a sl st in the top loop only of each ch. Fasten off. (10 sts)

Switch to CC3.

Row 3: With RS facing, make a sl st in the top loop only of each st. Fasten off, leaving a tail of approx 15cm (6in). (10 sts)

Tie

Using MC.

Make 80 ch. Fasten off. Fold tails of yarn on to chain and make a knot in each end, encompassing the tails of yarn. Trim the tails close to the knot.

Finishing

Sew the egg on to the bootie, place the egg slightly to the left on one bootie and slightly to the right on the other. The piece of bacon will form a loop through which you will feed the tie. Fold the piece of bacon in half and attach it over the back seam of the bootie using the light pink yarn ends. The bacon should not overlap with the bootie by more than 0.5cm (¼in). Thread the tie through the loop formed by the bacon.

HELPFUL TIPS

Any contrast colour will work as the MC yarn for these booties. You could also try using a different shade for the tie to add extra interest.

28
SCRUMPTIOUS
SUSHI

Wrap little feet in these stylish slippers, garnished with a prawn and secured with nori, just like traditional sushi.

BEFORE YOU BEGIN

SKILL LEVEL
2

YOU WILL NEED
Debbie Bliss Mia 50g (1.75oz); 100m (109yds); 50% cotton/ 50% wool
1 in White (01) = MC
Small amount of Peach (12) = CC1
Small amount of DK weight yarn in black = CC2

Hook
3.5mm (US E/4), for making the smaller size prawn
4mm (US G/6)
Adjust hook size if necessary to achieve correct tension

Notions
Stitch marker
Yarn needle

TENSION
10 sts and 10 rows in dc to measure 5cm (2in)

SIZES
0–6 months, sole length 9cm (3½in)
6–12 months, sole length 10cm (4in)

Note: Instructions are given for the smallest size first; the larger size is given in square brackets [ ]

STITCHES AND SKILLS
See Crochet Basics (pages 134–142)

Working in rows
Working in rounds
Working into front and back loops
dc2tog
dtr bobble

To Make the Booties

(make 2)

Toe

Using MC.

Round 1: Make 3[4] ch, 2 dc into 2nd ch from hook, 1 dc into next 0[1] ch, 4 dc into last ch, working into opposite side of ch, 1 dc into next 0[1] ch, 2 dc into ch that already contains 2 dc. (8[10] sts)

Round 2: 2 dc into next st, 1 dc into each of next 2[3] sts, 2 dc into each of next 2 sts, 1 dc into each of next 2[3] sts, 2 dc into last st. (12[14] sts)

HELPFUL TIP
Carry any unused colour up the inside of the work until it is needed again.

Round 3: 2 dc into next st, 1 dc into each of next 4[5] sts, 2 dc into each of next 2 sts, 1 dc into each of next 4[5] sts, 2 dc into last st. (16[18] sts)

Round 4: 2 dc into each of next 2 sts, 1 dc into each of next 6[7] sts, 2 dc into each of next 2 sts, 1 dc into each of next 6[7] sts. (20[22] sts)

Round 5: 1 dc into each st. (20[22] sts)

Rounds 6–10[11]: Rep Round 5. (20[22] sts)

Body

Note: Beg 1 ch is not counted as a st.

Row 1: 1 dc into each of next 16[17] sts, turn, leaving the rem 4[5] sts unworked. (16[17] sts)

Row 2: 1 ch, 1 dc into each of next 15[16] sts, turn, leaving rem st unworked. (15[16] sts)

Row 3: 1 ch, 1 dc into each st, turn. (15[16] sts)

Rows 4–11: Rep Row 3. (15[16] sts)

For larger size only: Rep Row 3 twice more. ([16] sts)

Back Seam

Fold the back seam in half with RS together. Working through flo of the piece closest to you and blo of the piece farthest away from you, join the two sides together by working a sl st though both layers into each of the next 7[8] sts. Fasten off and weave ends into WS.

HELPFUL TIP

The body is worked in rows, and the toes are worked in a spiral. Use the larger hook throughout except for the prawn for the smaller size.

Edging Rows

Round 1: With RS facing, work 26[31] dc evenly around the foot opening, working 1 dc into each row end and each st, sl st into first dc to join. (26[31] sts)

For larger size only: 1 ch, 1 dc into each st. ([31] sts)

Fasten off and weave ends into WS.

Prawn

For smaller size: use 3.5mm crochet hook

For larger size: use 4mm crochet hook

Prawn Body

Using CC1.

Round 1: Make 6 ch, 2 dc into 2nd ch from hook, 1 dc into each of next 3 sts, 4 dc into next st, working into opposite side of ch, 1 dc into each of next 3 sts, 2 dc into last st. (14 sts)

Cont to work in a spiral.

Round 2: 1 dc into each st, switch to MC. (14 sts)

Round 3: 1 dc into each st, switch to CC1. (14 sts)

Rounds 4–5: 1 dc into each st. (14 sts)

Round 6: Switch to MC. *Dc2tog, 1 dc into each of next 5 sts; rep from * once more, switch to CC1. (12 sts)

Rounds 7–8: 1 dc into each st. (12 sts)

Round 9: Switch to MC. *Dc2tog, 1 dc into each of next 4 sts; rep from * once more. (10 sts)

Round 10: *Dc2tog, 1 dc into each of next 3 sts; rep from * once more. (8 sts)

Sl st into next st and fasten off.

Prawn Tail

Using CC1.

Row 1: Close the last round by folding the prawn flat and working 3 dc across the open edge through both layers, turn.

Row 2: Work 1 dtr bobble into first st, 4 ch, sl st into same st, sl st into each of next 2 sts, work 1 dtr bobble into same (last) st, 4 ch, sl st in same st. Fasten off, leaving a tail of approx 20cm (8in). Wrap the yarn around the base of the tail 3 times and pull tight. Weave ends of yarn into WS.

Nori

Using CC2.

Leaving a 15cm (6in) initial tail of yarn, make 25[29] ch, 1 dc into the back bump of 2nd ch from hook, 1 dc into back bump of each rem ch. Fasten off, leaving a 15cm (6in) tail of yarn. (24[28] sts)

Finishing

Attach prawn and nori as follows: place the prawn on top of the bootie so that the tail hangs over the opening. Working through back layer of prawn only, sew it on to the bootie. Weave ends into WS. Thread one of the tails of yarn from the nori through the nori until you reach the middle. Leave this tail of yarn for sewing the nori to the bootie later. Thread the other tail of yarn and join the start and end of the nori to each other. Slip the nori over the bootie and the prawn (about halfway up the length of the prawn). Make sure that the seam of the nori is at the bottom of the bootie. Use backstitch to attach the nori to the bottom of the bootie and weave yarn ends into WS. Use the rem tail of yarn to attach the nori to the top of the prawn and weave ends into WS.

29
PEAS IN A POD

Keep little feet as snug as peas in a pod with these adorable slippers. For added cuteness, embroider a smiley face on to one of the peas.

BEFORE YOU BEGIN

SKILL LEVEL
1

YOU WILL NEED
Sirdar Snuggly Baby Bamboo DK
50g (1.75oz); 95m (104yds); 80% bamboo/20% wool
1 in Willow (133) = MC
Small amount of Limey (155) = CC1

Hook
3.5mm (US E/4)
Adjust hook size if necessary to achieve correct tension

Notions
2 stitch markers
Yarn needle

TENSION
9 sts and 11 rows in dc to measure 5cm (2in)

SIZES
0–6 months, sole length 9cm (3½in)
6–12 months, sole length 10cm (4in)

Note: Instructions are given for the smallest size first; the larger size is given in square brackets [ ]

STITCHES AND SKILLS
See Crochet Basics (pages 134–142)

Working in rows
Working in rounds
dc2tog

NOTES
The bootie is made from toe to heel.
Foot is worked in rows. Beg 1 ch is not counted as a st.
The peas and finishing edge are the same for both sizes.

To Make the Booties

(make 2)

Toe

Using MC.
Round 1: Make 2 ch, 3 dc into 2nd ch from hook. (3 sts)

Cont to work in a spiral.

Rounds 2–3: 1 dc into each st. (3 sts)

Round 4: 2 dc into each st. (6 sts)

Round 5: *1 dc into next st, 2 dc into next st; rep from * twice more, turn. (9 sts)

Cont in rows for foot.

Row 6: 1 ch, *1 dc into each of next 2 sts, 2 dc into next st; rep from * twice more, turn. (12 sts)

Row 7: 1 ch, *1 dc into each of next 3 sts, 2 dc into next st, rep from * twice more, turn. (15 sts)

Row 8: 1 ch, *1 dc into each of next 4 sts, 2 dc into next st, rep from * twice more, turn. (18 sts)

For larger size only: 1 ch, *1 dc into each of next 5 sts, 2 dc into next st, rep from * twice more, turn. ([21 sts])

Rows 9–21[10–23]: 1 ch, 1 dc into each st, turn. (18[21] sts)

Row 22[24]: 1 ch, 1 dc into each of next 5[6] sts, dc2tog 4 times, 1 dc into each of next 5[6] sts, turn. (14[17] sts)

Row 23[25]: 1 ch, 1 dc into each of next 3[5] sts, dc2tog 4 times, 1 dc into each of next 3[4] sts, turn. (10[13] sts)

Row 24[26]: 1 ch, 1 dc into each of next 1[2] st(s), dc2tog 4 times, 1 dc into each of next 1[3] sts, sl st into first dc to join, turn. (6[9] sts)

Round 25[27]: 1 ch, 1 dc into each of next 2[1] st(s), dc2tog 2[4] times. (4[5] sts)

Cont to work in a spiral.

Rounds 26–28[28–29]: 1 dc into each st. (4[5] sts)

Round 29[30]: 1 dc into each of next 2[1] st(s), dc2tog 1[2] times. (3[3] sts)

Fasten off. Weave ends into WS.

Peas

(make 3 per bootie)

Using CC1.
Round 1: Make 2 ch, 4 dc into 2nd ch from hook. (4 sts)

Cont to work in a spiral.

Round 2: 2 dc into each st. (8 sts)

Rounds 3–4: 1 dc into each st. (8 sts)

Sl st into the first st of last round to finish. Fasten off, weave ends into WS. Using CC1, sew 3 peas together in a row. Next, using CC1 sew the peas into the inside of the slipper toe.

Finishing

Round 1: Using a sl st, join MC to the centre back of the foot opening, 1 ch, work 1 dc into each row end along edge to the peas, skip across the peas and work in the same way along edge to centre back, sl st to first st to join.

Locate the pea at the opposite side of the foot opening. The 2 dc of the edging are the centre. Count 6 sts either side and mark both with a stitch marker.

Round 2: Sl st into each st of edging until you reach the first stitch marker, 4 ch, sl st to the second stitch marker, sl st into each st of edging to centre back, sl st into first sl st to join. Fasten off. Weave in ends.

30

TROPICAL WATERMELON

HELPFUL TIP

For even placement of seeds, start with one at the centre and then place two evenly on each side. Use an embroidered chain stitch as follows: bring yarn through fabric, then back into the same sp, come back up approx 1.25cm (½in) away, catching a loop with the needle, then go back down into a space very close to the first st.

Add a splash of summer to your baby's wardrobe with these cute sandal inspired booties. Refresh little toes with a slice of juicy watermelon.

BEFORE YOU BEGIN

SKILL LEVEL
1

YOU WILL NEED
Cascade 220 Sport 50g (1.75oz); 150m (164yds); 100% Peruvian highland wool
1 in Christmas Green (8894) = MC
Small amount of DK weight yarn in white = CC1
1 in Flamingo Pink (7805) = CC2

Hook
3.75mm (US F/5)
Adjust hook size if necessary to achieve correct tension

Notions
Black yarn or embroidery thread
Stitch markers
Yarn needle

TENSION
11 sts and 8 rows in htr to measure 5cm (2in)

SIZES
0–6 months, sole length 9cm (3½in)
6–12 months, sole length 10cm (4in)

Note: Instructions are given for the smallest size first; the larger size is given in square brackets [ ]

STITCHES AND SKILLS
See Crochet Basics (pages 134–142)

Sole 1
Working in rows
Working in rounds
dc2tog
htr2tog

NOTES
CC2 yarn used in photograph in Shrimp (7804), discontinued.

To Make the Booties
(make 2)

Sole
Using MC, make Sole 1. (46[50] sts)

Do not fasten off, cont with sides.

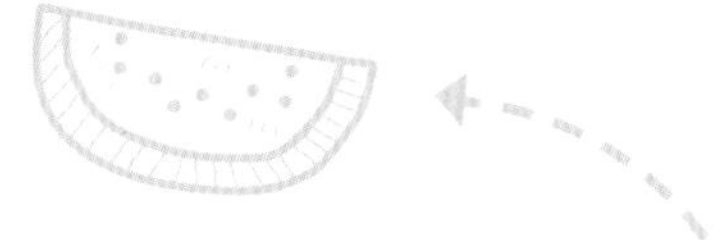

Sides
Using MC.

Round 1–2: 1 ch, 1 htr into same st, 1 htr into each rem st, sl st into first htr to join. (46[50] sts)

Fasten off, leaving a tail of approx 20cm (8in). Using stitch markers, mark the front and back centre of the slipper bottom between 2 sts. The front half of the slipper will be worked over 28[30] sts, the back half over the rem 18[20] sts.

Front

Attach CC1 to 14th[15th] st to the right of centre front of shoe.

Row 1: 1 ch, 1 dc into same st, 1 dc into each of next 27[29] sts, cut yarn and fasten off. (28[30] sts)

Join CC2 with a sl st into first dc worked in CC1.

Row 2: 1 ch, 1 htr into each of first 4[5] sts, *htr2tog, 1 htr into next st; rep from * 5 more times, htr2tog, 1 htr into each of next 4[5] sts, turn. (21[23] sts)

Row 3: 1 ch, 1 htr into each of first 4[5] sts, htr2tog 3 times, 1 htr into next st, htr2tog 3 times, 1 htr into each of last 4[5] sts, turn. (15[17] sts)

Row 4: 1 ch, 1 htr into each of first 3[4] sts, htr2tog twice, 1 htr into next st, htr2tog twice, 1 htr into each of last 3[4] sts, turn. (11[13] sts)

Row 5: 1 ch, 1 htr into each of first 3[4] sts, htr2tog, 1 htr into next st, htr2tog, 1 htr into each of last 3[4] sts. (9[11] sts)

Fasten off, leaving a tail of approx 30cm (12in). Fold the final row in half and whipstitch it together, using the tail of yarn.

Back

Attach MC with a sl st directly to the left of last dc worked in CC1 (Row 1).

Row 1: 1 ch, 1 htr into same st, htr2tog, 1 htr into each of next 12[14] sts, htr2tog, 1 htr into last st, turn. (16[18] sts)

Row 2: 1 ch, 1 htr into same st, htr2tog, 1 htr into each of next 10[12] sts, htr2tog, 1 htr into last st, turn. (14[16] sts)

Row 3: 1 ch, 1 dc into first st, dc2tog, 1 dc into each of next 3[4] sts, dc2tog, 1 dc into each of next 3[4] sts, dc2tog, 1 dc into last st, 3 ch, 1 dc into each side of Rows 3–5 of slipper front, dc2tog into both sides of Row 5 of slipper front (across the seam), 1 dc into the other half of the side of Row 5 and into Rows 4–3, 3 ch, sl st into first dc of Row 3 of slipper back. Fasten off, weave ends into WS.

Finishing

Using black yarn or thread, embroider 5 watermelon seeds on to the top of the front of shoe. For best results, work across the 2nd and 3rd rows of CC2.

CROCHET BASICS

Before you start crocheting, gather together everything you will need for your project. Read over the pattern before you begin. If you are new to crochet, read over the basic skills and techniques covered in this chapter before picking up your hook. Have fun crocheting!

Crochet Equipment

Items you will need to complete patterns in this book include: crochet hooks, stitch markers, scissors, yarn, pins, a ruler and a yarn needle. Other more unusual supplies will be listed within each pattern.

Crochet Hooks

Crochet hooks are made from a variety of materials. They come in different shapes and sizes and some have large, chunky handles that are ergonomically designed for comfort when crocheting. It is important to choose a crochet hook that feels comfortable to use.

Each project lists the size(s) of hook needed for that pattern. Always use the size of hook stated and check the tension before starting your project (see Getting Started, page 137). Change the hook size as necessary to obtain the correct tension so that the shoes will be finished to the correct size.

Note: There is no US size equivalent for UK hook sizes 2.5mm and 3mm, so use either one hook size smaller, or one hook size larger:

- For 2.5 mm use either US B/1 or C/2
- For 3 mm use either US C/2 or D/3

Stitch Markers and Pins

Stitch markers are used to mark specific stitches in a pattern. If you do not have access to ready-made markers, use a piece of scrap yarn or even a safety pin to mark the stitch. Pins may be useful when sewing different sections together.

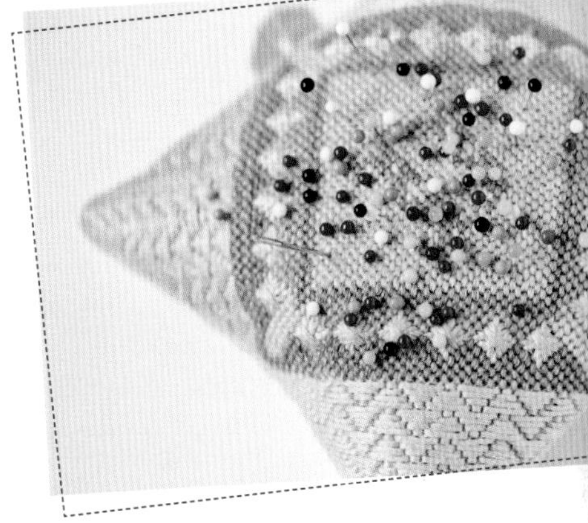

Ruler or Size Gauge

A ruler or size gauge can be used to test the sample swatch tension before you begin your project and to measure the final project when finished.

Yarn Needle

The yarn needle is used to sew the different pieces together and for weaving in ends.

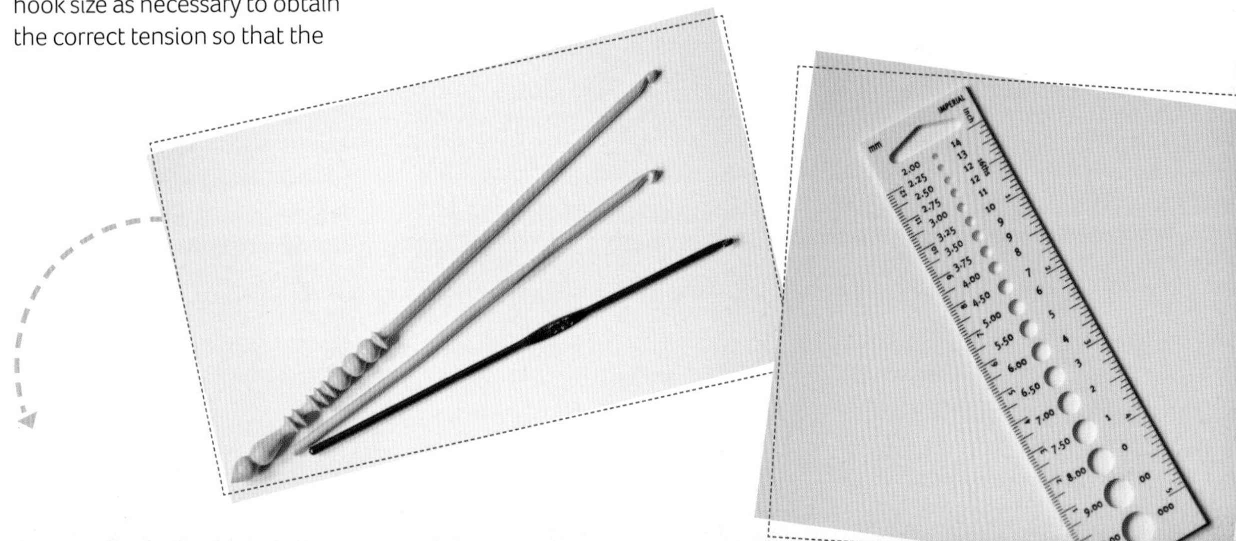

How to Read the Patterns

If you are new to reading patterns, you may feel that they are written in a different language. However, you will soon begin to recognise the abbreviations used. Here are some key pointers for reading crochet patterns:

- When a number appears before the stitch name, such as 3 htr, work these stitches into the same stitch, for example, '3 tr into next st'.
- When only one stitch is to be worked into each of a number of stitches, it can be written like this, for example, '1 tr into each of next 3 sts'. When a number appears after a chain, for example, ch3, this means work the number of chains indicated.
- The number in parentheses ( ) at the end of a round or row gives the total number of stitches for that round or row and helps you keep track of progress.
- The asterisks mark a specific set of instructions that are repeated, for example '*2 dc into next st, 1 dc into next st; rep from * to end' means repeat the stitches between the asterisk and the semi-colon.
- When instructions are written within a set of parentheses, it can mean two things, for example '(1 dc, 1 tr, 1 dc) all into the next stitch' means work 1 dc, 1 tr, 1 dc all into the same stitch and it can also mean a set of stitches repeated a number of times, for example, '(2dc into next st) 5 times'.

Crochet Abbreviations:

approx	approximately
beg	begin(ning)
blo	back loop only
bphtr	back post half treble crochet
bptr	back post treble crochet
ch	chain
cont	continue
dc	double crochet
dec	decrease
dc2tog	double crochet next 2 sts together to decrease 1 st
dc3tog	double crochet next 3 sts together to decrease 2 sts
dtr	double treble crochet
flo	front loop only
fptr	front post treble crochet
fphtr	front post half treble crochet
htr	half treble crochet
htr2tog	half treble crochet next 2 sts together to decrease 1 st
rem	remain(ing)
rep	repeat
RS	right side
sl st	slip stitch
slst2tog	slip stitch next 2 sts together to decrease 1 st
sp	space
st(s)	stitch(es)
tr	treble crochet
tr2tog	treble crochet next 2 sts together to decrease 1 st
tr6tog	treble crochet next 6 sts together to decrease 5 sts
WS	wrong side
MC	main colour
CC	contrast colour

Anatomy of a Stitch

Each crochet stitch consists of a vertical post and a set of two horizontal loops across the top which form a 'V' shape, with one front loop and one back loop. Unless specified otherwise, you will insert the hook under both horizontal 'V'-shaped loops to crochet any stitch.

Finding the Stitch Post

The vertical bar or section right below the top of the stitch is called the post. You will use this part of the stitch when crocheting front post or back post stitches.

Using Front Loop Only and Back Loop Only

When instructed to use the front loop only (flo), you will use the loop closest to you – this is the 'front' of the stitch. When instructed to use the back loop only (blo), you will use the loop furthest from you – this is the 'back' of the stitch.

Getting Started

How to Hold the Hook

There are two common ways to hold the hook: pencil style and knife style. Try both holds and see which one you prefer.

Pencil Style Hold the hook in your hand as you would hold a pencil between your thumb and forefinger.

Knife Style Place your hand over the hook with the handle resting against the palm and thumb, and place your index finger on the thumb rest.

How to Hold Yarn

Like holding the hook, there are two different ways to hold the yarn when crocheting. Choose the one that is most comfortable. Pay attention to yarn tension – how tightly you are pulling on the yarn – as this will affect the tension. You want to maintain an even yarn tension, which will yield a fabric with evenly sized stitches, not too loose and not too tight.

Over the Little Finger Hold
Wrap the yarn over your hand and around your little finger.

Over the Middle Finger Hold
Wrap the yarn around your middle finger and over your index finger to guide the yarn.

Checking Tension

The key to crocheting booties that fit correctly is to check the tension before you start. Every pattern in this book tells you the tension for that project, namely how many stitches and rows per 5cm (2in) of a piece of fabric the final measurements were based on.

To check tension, you need to crochet a sample swatch using the yarn, hook size and crochet stitch specified. Crochet the swatch at least 2.5cm (1in) larger than required so that you can check the stitches and rows within the swatch to ensure the correct tension. For instance, if the tension is determined to be 5cm (2in) square in double crochet, you will work up a swatch in dc at least 7.5cm (3in) square. Lay a measuring tape on the swatch and count across how many stitches you have in 5cm (2in). Now reposition the tape and measure up and down how many rows you have in 5cm (2in).

If you have more stitches and rows than stated, the tension is too tight and the stitches are too small. Try using a hook one size larger than recommended in the pattern and make another tension swatch. If necessary, keep doing this until the swatch matches the pattern tension. If you have fewer stitches and rows than stated, the tension is too loose and the stitches are too big. Try using a hook one size smaller than recommended in the pattern and make another tension swatch. If necessary, repeat until the swatch matches the pattern tension.

Counting Stitches

To count stitches, look at the top of the row. The finished horizontal 'V' shaped stitches look like joined teardrops. Each one is considered a stitch. Use stitch markers to mark the first and last stitch of each row.

Changing Colours

When you are working in double crochet and switching yarns in a piece, use this technique for a clean colour change: insert the hook into the next stitch and pull the yarn back through the stitch. Yarn over with the next colour and pull through. The colour change is complete. Cut the yarn for the original colour, leaving a few centimetres.

If you are working a colour change for a half treble crochet, treble crochet or double treble crochet, complete the stitch until the last pull through. Yarn over with the next colour and pull through to complete the colour change.

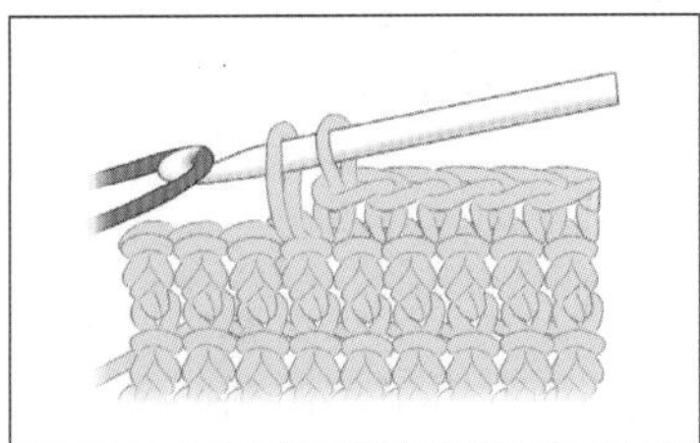

Changing colours

Crocheting in Rows

When working in rows, you will be working back and forth across the work. When finishing the end of a row you will turn and work the next row according to the pattern.

Crocheting in the Round

Crocheting 'in the round' means that you will be working in one direction throughout, not back and forth in rows. There are two ways you can work in the round:

Joined Rounds If you are working in joined rounds, the round will be joined with a slip stitch to complete the round. You will then start a new round using the same number of chains as the turning chain for that stitch, for example 1 ch for a double crochet, and this round will then be joined with a slip stitch into the first chain.

Continuous Rounds If you are working in continuous rounds, the rounds will move smoothly from one to the next without joining (like a spiral). Use a stitch marker to mark the first stitch of the round so that you know when you have reached the end of the round. Move the stitch marker after each round is complete.

Turning

When you are working in dc, 1 ch is worked at the start of every row. This is called a turning chain and it brings the hook up to the correct height of the stitches being worked. The double crochet turning chain does not count as a stitch. For other stitch types the turning chain is longer and also counts as a stitch. The turning chain for these stitches are listed below:

half treble crochet = 2 ch
treble crochet = 3 ch
double treble crochet = 4 ch
triple treble crochet = 5 ch

Right Side and Wrong Side

When working in rows, the right side will be Row 1 unless otherwise stated. When working 'in the round' the right side will be the side facing you when completing the stitch. The wrong side will be on the opposite side.

Fastening Off

When you reach the end of your crochet project, you will need to fasten off the yarn. To fasten off, simply cut the yarn, leaving a few centimetres (unless otherwise instructed), and draw the yarn through the last loop on the hook. Pull yarn tight to secure the knot.

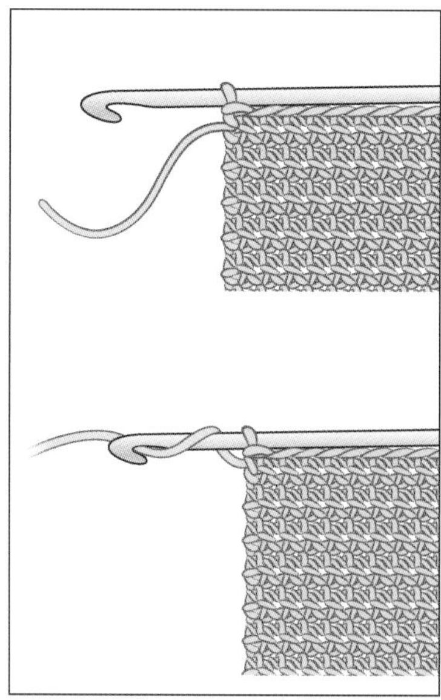

Fastening off

Weaving in Ends

Use the hook or a yarn needle to weave any cut ends up and down through 3 or 4 stitches (at least). After weaving, trim the end as close to the crocheted piece as possible to hide it.

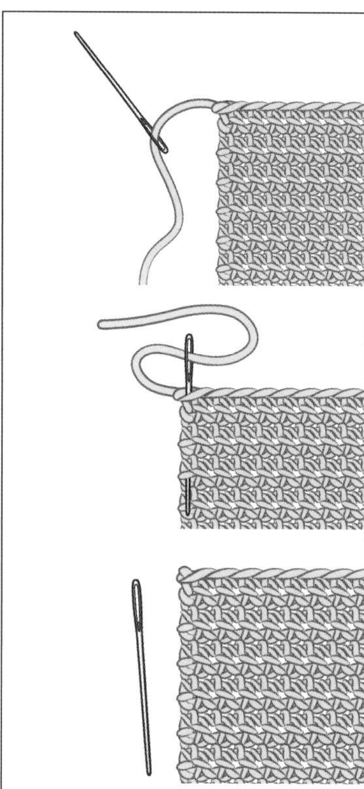

Weaving in ends

Joining Seams

Backstitch is ideal for stitching seams together. Working right to left, bring the needle up through the work and make a stitch going to the right. Now bring up the needle to the left of the beginning of the first stitch, at stitch-length distance. Make a stitch going to the right, which meets the start of the first stitch. Repeat to the end of the row.

Stitch Guide

Magic Loop

Loop the yarn around your fingers with the yarn tail on the left and the working yarn on the right. Insert the hook though the ring and pull a loop from the working yarn. Make 1 chain and then make the required number of stitches around the ring and the yarn tail. Pull the yarn tail to close the ring and join with a slip stitch into the first stitch.

Slip Knot

Make a loop in the yarn. With the crochet hook or your finger, grab the yarn from the ball and pull through the loop. Pull tight on the yarn and adjust to create first loop.

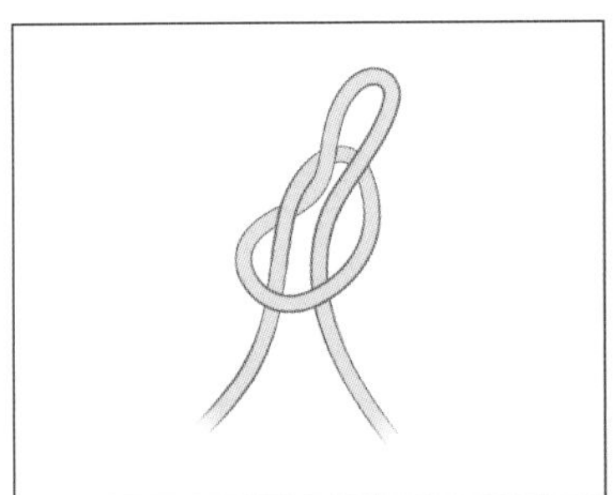

Slip knot

Chain (ch)

The chain provides the foundation for your stitches at the beginning of a pattern. It can also serve as a stitch within a pattern and be used to create an open effect or loops.

Make a slip knot and place it on to the hook. Wind the yarn over the hook. Keeping the yarn taut but not too tight (see Tip, below), pull the yarn downwards through the slip knot. Chain 1 is complete and is sitting directly below the hook. Next, *wind the yarn over the hook and pull the yarn through the loop on the hook. Chain 2 is complete. Repeat from * to create multiple chains.

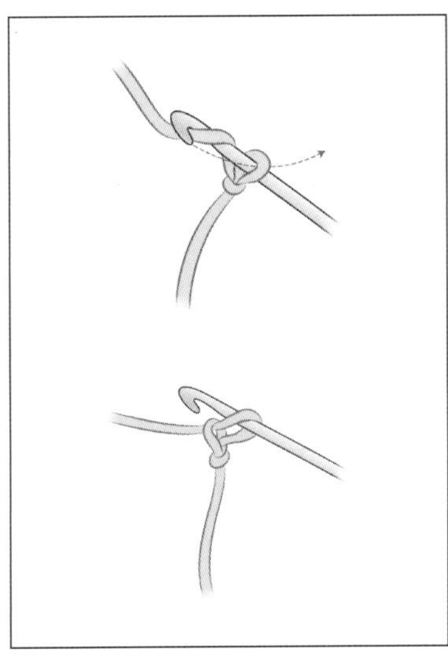

Chain

Slip Stitch (sl st)

This stitch is used to join one stitch to another or to join a stitch to another point.

Insert the hook into the next stitch from front to back and yarn over, just as for a chain stitch. Pull the yarn back through the stitch: 2 loops on hook. Continue to pull the yarn through the original loop on the hook to complete.

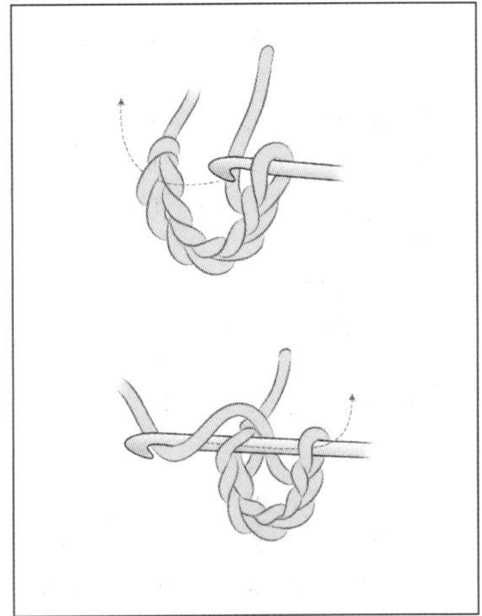

Slip stitch

Slip Stitch 2 Together (slst2tog)

Insert hook into the next stitch, yarn over and pull back through stitch: 2 loops on hook. Insert hook into the next stitch, yarn over and pull back through stitch and also through 2 loops on hook to complete.

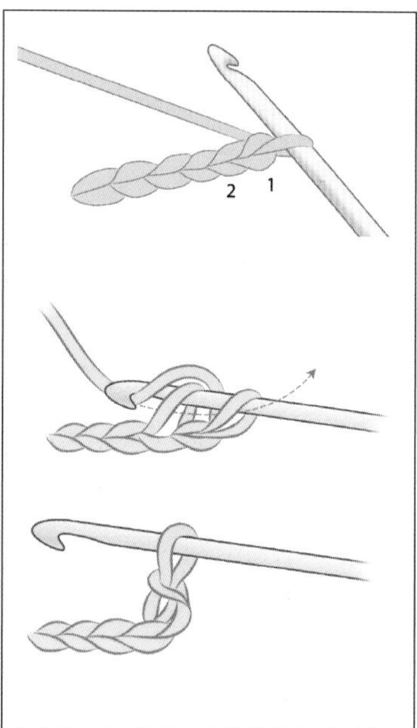

Double crochet

Half Treble Crochet (htr)
Yarn over and insert the hook into the next stitch, from the front of the stitch to the back. Yarn over and pull yarn back through the stitch: 3 loops on hook. Yarn over and draw through all 3 loops on hook to complete.

Treble Crochet (tr)
Yarn over and insert the hook into the next stitch, from the front of the stitch to the back. Yarn over and pull the yarn back through the stitch: 3 loops on hook. Yarn over and draw the yarn through the first 2 loops on the hook: 2 loops on hook. Yarn over and draw the yarn through the last 2 loops on hook to complete.

Double Crochet (dc)
Insert the hook into the next stitch, from the front of the stitch to the back and yarn over. Pull the yarn back through the stitch: 2 loops on hook. Yarn over and draw through both loops on the hook to complete.

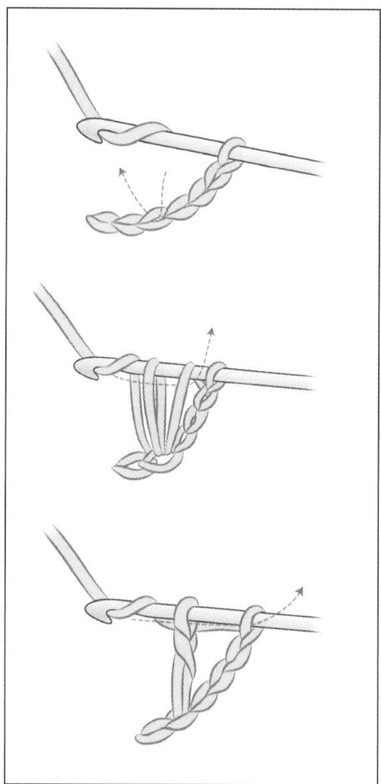
Treble crochet

Double Treble Crochet (dtr)
Yarn over twice and insert the hook into the next stitch, from the front of the stitch to the back. Yarn over and pull the yarn back through the stitch: 4 loops on hook. Yarn over and draw the yarn through the first 2 loops on the hook: 3 loops on hook. Yarn over and draw the yarn through the next 2 loops on the hook: 2 loops on hook. Yarn over and draw the yarn through the last 2 loops on hook to complete.

Front Post Half Treble Crochet (fphtr)
Yarn over and insert the hook from the front to the back to the front of the next stitch around the post (see Anatomy of a Stitch, page 136, for where the post is located). Yarn over and pull the yarn back around the post: 3 loops on hook. Yarn over and draw the yarn through all loops on hook to complete.

Back Post Half Treble Crochet (bphtr)
Yarn over and insert the hook from the back to the front to the back of the next stitch around the post (see Anatomy of a Stitch, page 136, for where the post is located). Yarn over and pull the yarn back around the post: 3 loops on hook. Yarn over and draw the yarn through all loops on hook to complete.

Front Post Treble Crochet (fptr)

Yarn over and insert the hook from the front to the back to the front of the next stitch around the post (see Anatomy of a Stitch panel, page 136, for where the post is located). Yarn over and pull the yarn back around the post: 3 loops on hook. Yarn over and draw the yarn through the first 2 loops on the hook: 2 loops on hook. Yarn over and draw the yarn through last 2 loops on hook to complete.

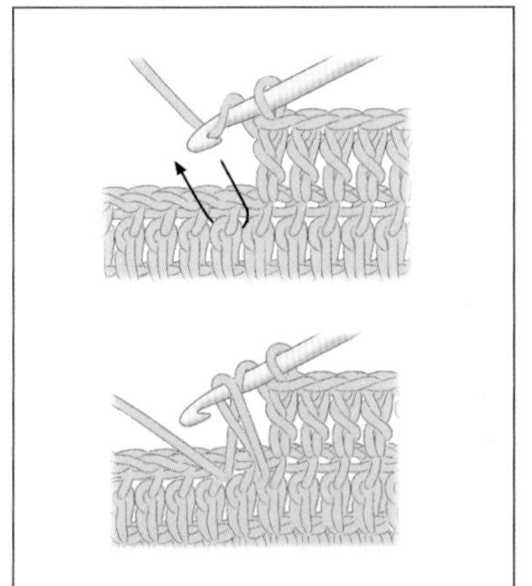

Front post treble crochet

Back Post Treble Crochet (bptr)

Yarn over and insert the hook from the back to the front to the back of the next stitch around the post (see Anatomy of a Stitch panel, page 136, for where the post is located). Yarn over and pull the yarn back around the post: 3 loops on hook. Yarn over and draw the yarn through the first 2 loops on hook: 2 loops on hook. Yarn over and draw the yarn through last 2 loops on hook to complete.

Double Crochet Decrease (dc2tog)

A double crochet decrease 2 together will take two stitches and make them into one double crochet stitch.

Insert the hook into the next stitch, from the front of the stitch to the back and yarn over. Pull the yarn back through the stitch: 2 loops on hook. Leaving the loops on the hook, insert the hook from front to back into the next stitch. Yarn over and pull back through stitch: 3 loops on hook. Yarn over and draw through all 3 loops on the hook to complete.

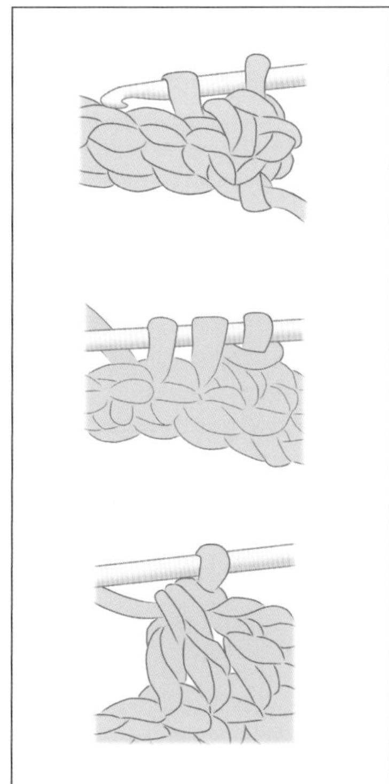

Double crochet decrease

Double Crochet Invisible Decrease (invdec)

A double crochet invisible decrease will take two stitches and make them into one double crochet through the front loop only (flo).

Insert the hook into flo of the next stitch and yarn over. Pull the yarn back through: 2 loops on hook. Leaving the loops on the hook, insert the hook into flo of the next stitch. Yarn over and pull back through stitch: 3 loops on hook. Yarn over and draw through all 3 loops on the hook to complete.

Double Crochet 3 Together (dc3tog)

A double crochet decrease 3 together will take three stitches and make them into one double crochet stitch.

Insert the hook into the next stitch, from the front of the stitch to the back and yarn over. Pull the yarn back through the stitch: 2 loops on hook. Leaving the loops on the hook, insert the hook from front to back into the next stitch. Yarn over and pull back though stitch: 3 loops on hook. Leaving the loops on the hook, insert the hook from front to back into the next stitch. Yarn over and pull back through stitch: 4 loops on hook. Yarn over and draw through all 4 loops on hook to complete.

Half Treble Crochet Decrease (htr2tog)

A half treble crochet decrease will take two stitches and make them into one half treble crochet stitch.

Yarn over and insert the hook into the next stitch, from the front of the stitch to the back. Yarn over and pull yarn back through stitch: 3 loops on hook. Yarn over and insert hook from front to back into the next stitch. Yarn over and pull yarn back through stitch: 5 loops on hook. Yarn over and pull yarn through all 5 loops on hook to complete.

Treble Crochet Decrease (tr2tog)

A treble crochet decrease will take two stitches and make them into one treble crochet stitch.

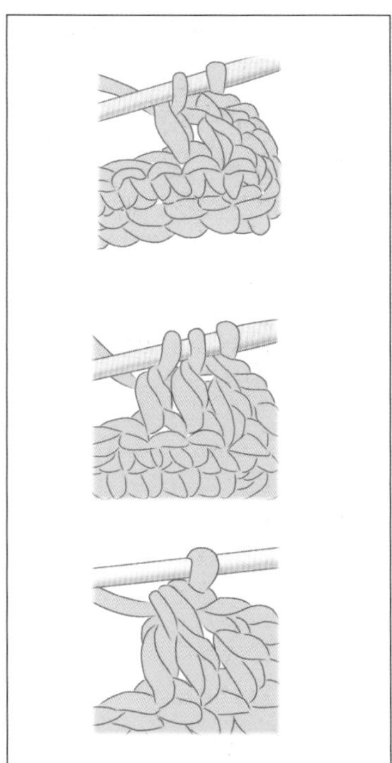

Treble crochet decrease

Yarn over and insert the hook into the next stitch, from the front of the stitch to the back. Yarn over and pull the yarn back through the stitch: 3 loops on hook. Yarn over and draw the yarn through the first 2 loops on the hook: 2 loops on hook. Leaving the loops on the hook, insert the hook front to back into the next stitch. Yarn over and pull back through the stitch: 4 loops on hook. Yarn over and draw the yarn through the first 2 loops on the hook: 3 loops on hook. Yarn over and draw the yarn through all 3 loops on hook to complete.

Treble Crochet 6 Together (tr6tog)

A treble crochet 6 together will take six stitches and make them into one treble crochet stitch.

*Yarn over, insert hook into the next stitch, yarn over and draw it back through the stitch (3 loops on hook), yarn over and pull through the first 2 loops on hook (2 loops left on hook); rep from * 5 more times (7 loops on hook), yarn over and pull through all 7 loops to complete.

Crab Stitch

Insert hook into the next stitch to the right of the hook (instead of left), from front to back and with the hook pointing downwards. Yarn over hook and draw it back through the stitch: 2 loops on hook. Yarn over hook and pull through both loops on hook to complete.

Loop Stitch

Wrap the yarn from front to back over your index finger. The length of the loop will depend on how loose or tight you wrap the yarn in this step. Insert the hook into the next stitch, grab the strand of yarn from behind finger, and draw the yarn through the stitch. The yarn on the finger becomes the loop. With the yarn loop still on the index finger, yarn over and pull the yarn through the 2 loops on hook. Make sure that all the loops are the same length in order to achieve a finished look.

Double Treble Bobble (Dtr Bobble)

4 ch, yarn over twice and insert hook into the same stitch, * yarn over and pull through 2 loops, rep from * one more time, yarn over twice and insert hook into same stitch. ** Yarn over and pull through 2 loops, rep from ** one more time: 3 loops on hook. Yarn over and pull through all 3 loops on the hook to complete.

Shell

Each Shell falls over 3 stitches.

(Htr, tr) into next st, 2 ch, sl st into the second chain from the hook to form a picot. (Tr, htr) into next st. Sl st into next st.

Soles

The projects in this book either start with making a sole or are worked from toe-to-heel. There are two sole templates used for the shoes with a sole base: Sole 1 and Sole 2. For either sole, at the end of each round, join with a sl st into the first htr and then start the next round working into the next stitch, not into the stitch with the sl st. Follow the instructions for each project to see whether or not to fasten off after completing the sole.

How to Make SOLE 1

To fit ages:

- 0–6 months, sole length 9cm (3½in)
- 6–12 months, sole length 10cm (4in)

Changes for size 6–12 months are in [ ]

Round 1: Make 11 [13] ch, 1 htr into 3rd ch from hook, 1 htr into each of next 7[9] sts, 6 htr into last ch, work on opposite side, 1 htr into each of next 7[9] sts, 5 htr into last ch, join with sl st into first htr.

Round 2: 1 ch, 1 htr into each of next 8[10] sts, 2 htr into each of next 5 sts, 1 htr into each of next 8[10] sts, 2 htr into each of next 5 sts, join with sl st into first htr.

Round 3: 1 ch, 1 htr into each of next 8[10] sts, (2 htr into next st, 1 hdc into next st) 5 times, 1 htr into each of next 8[10] sts, (2 htr into next st, 1 hdc into next st) 5 times, join with sl st into first htr. (46[50] sts)

How to Make SOLE 2

To fit ages:

- 0–6 months, sole length 9cm (3½in)
- 6–12 months, sole length 10cm (4in)

Changes for size 6–12 months are in [ ]

Round 1: Make 9[11] ch, 1 htr into 3rd ch from hook, 1 htr into each of next 5[7] sts, 6 htr into last ch, work on opposite side, 1 htr into each of next 5[7] sts, 5 htr into last ch, join with sl st into first htr.

Round 2: 1 ch, 1 htr into each of next 6[8] sts, 2 htr into each of next 5 sts, 1 htr into each of next 6[8] sts, 2 htr into each of next 5 sts, join with sl st into first htr.

Round 3: 1 ch, 1 htr into each of next 6[8] sts, (2 htr into next st, 1 htr into next st) 5 times, 1 htr into each of next 6[8] sts, (2 htr into next st, 1 htr into next st) 5 times, join with sl st into first htr. (42[46] sts)

Sole 1

Sole 2

Quantum Books would like to thank our lovely models:

Sophie Bloom
Edie Gaskell
Oscar LeCouffe
Caitlin McGlynn
Freya Workman

And their very helpful Mummies:

Colette Bloom
Kate Gaskell
Juliet LeCouffe
Lisa McDonald
Helen Workman

Thanks also to Lynne Rowe and Claire Crompton for their technical expertise.

Index